Dancing
Into
Joy

By M. Kathleen Chesnut

Dancing Into Joy

Transforming Our Darkness into Light

By M. Kathleen Chesnut

DewSpirit Publishing
Dickinson, North Dakota

DewSpirit
Publishing

Published in the United States by
DewSpirit Publishing, Dickinson, North Dakota
DewSpirit.com

Cover: cover design by Irene Archer, www.book-cover-design.com
author photograph by Ron Sticka Photography, Dickinson, ND

Publisher's Cataloging-in-Publication
(Provided by Quality Books, Inc.)

Chesnut, M. Kathleen.
    Dancing into joy : "Transforming Our Darkness into Light" / M.
Kathleen Chesnut.
    p. cm.
    LCCN 2006903049
    ISBN 0-9785090-0-5

    1. Chesnut, M. Kathleen. 2. Resurrection--Literary
collections. 3. Spiritual biography. 4. Meditations.
5. Spiritual life.   I. Title.

BV4832.3.C54 2006   242
                          QBI06-600123

Dedicated to all those who helped me find the joy that was hiding in my heart and the courage to go find it. May you, too, find that source of joy.

Table of Contents

Dancing into Joy: Transforming Our Darkness into Light

Prelude

When I was thirty-one, I came out of a depression that I had been in since I was five. The very air seemed different; the world expanded and became more intimate at the same time. Life felt new, was new. Then I grew depressed again as I mourned all that had been absent from my life. But I decided I would experience life as fully as God intended, no matter how much pain, how much unraveling was necessary to be able to do that. A year later I wrote the following poem:

And I Shall Dance this Way Again

I have walked this way before,
> but then the sun was hidden
> the earth was frozen
> the air was stiff and dead.
I walked enclosed in winter
> through which I had not chosen to travel
> into which I had been thrown
> unclothed, broken, five-years-old, alone.

A winter of years, not days,
A winter of years to teach distrust,
> of loss to teach emptiness,
> of terror to teach silence.
A winter peopled with icicles of anger
> snowdrifts of pain engulfing,
> survived, not felt.
The desire to destroy that which had hurt so much
> refused entry to my heart
> but controlling in a frozen fight.

But not quite.
At the core of my heart a spark of love
responded to a voice at the core of my soul
a voice I held onto in faith and believed
even when I did not believe in myself.

The voice I held to spoke of other things
      I listened-
      I followed-
hesitating, frightened, but accepting the help I was
      shown,
help readily given which slowly transformed my life.

At thirty-one I awoke one day
hearing a song so new I cried with joy-
the song of life that we were born to hear-
that we were born to sing.

I have walked this way before, but-
      not with so light a step upon an earth
      breathing with rain-washed life,
      not with the sun warm upon
      my back and shining in my heart.

And I shall walk, no-run, no- dance this way again.
For I have let people love and heal and touch me-
For I have learned to love and touch and grow.
And if the sun does not then shine,
No Matter

For I will have it glowing within me
singing and healing and growing in joy.

As you may have guessed, I had a really nasty childhood. Part of me was embraced by God's love when I was five and stayed connected to that experience of God; another part experienced great abuse and hid.

For quite some time, I have worked to unite the two parts, as the promise of God's love has become more real to all of me and has vanquished the fear and anger bequeathed to me by my childhood. This book is a gift for anyone who may be afraid, filled with writings I have done to express my journey of healing. It is my way of saying thanks to God – and to those people God placed in my path to remind me that people also know how to love. Written at different times as my first attempt at a book was in 1989, they show the opening up of my life as the darkness that I once lived in withdrew. I pray that they chase away some of the darkness that inhabits your life

The presence of God is singing in my heart this day. That presence of God has asked me to share my stories with you, and I do so. I share my stories of my life and my stories of fiction that hold more truth in a different way. I share my meditations that lead towards light and away from fear. I share my poetry and my prose poems, all of which underline the confidence I have in the presence of God's love in the substance of my life.

Dancing into Joy: Transforming Our Darkness into Light

Movement One - Faith

Without faith, many of us would be unable to get out of bed. Faith allows us to face the world with the expectation that it all will have been worth it at the end of the day. Faith in God, faith in other people, in our friends both human and animal, this is what permits us to face whatever fears we may have, to go forward and to live fully each day. And so I begin this gift of story with faith.

The Struggle to Believe - my story - 1989

I remember describing faith to friends some years ago. I imagined myself following a path and coming to a high cliff where the path ended. Below, a wild, rocky river cuts its way through rock and everything living. To continue to grow and heal, I knew I had to continue. But all my senses and previous knowledge told me I would fall, would be crushed. If I didn't die, the very least that would happen was that I would become a horrible cripple.

I could not see the other side where the path was presumed to continue. It could be that the path ended - a horrible joke played on one stupid enough to trust - again. I looked into the distance, trying to see, and was only aware of the jagged, broken rocks below.

I felt like a cripple anyway. When with people at that time, I was overcome with fear, terror of what they could do to harm me washing up from the terrors of my childhood. Fear dug a chasm between others and myself, separating me from those I wished to learn to trust.

Faced with this chasm, I had only faith to guide me, faith in the voice I heard speaking to me, telling me to trust, faith that the voice was God, faith in God.

When I was five, I had felt the overwhelming power of the love that Jesus had for me, love so strong that it wiped out everything my mother had taught me about her version of love - her version which said that if you love someone, you must let them use you as they will - that love entailed possessing, controlling. But this love washed away much of that pain, for the love I felt from Jesus does not, never will, use anyone or anything.

But standing at the edge of the chasm, I found it difficult to remember this. As I had yet to remember the experience that caused me to call for help to God, I had yet to remember the results of that call - the experience of being bathed in love and that love consuming my pain and brokenness, "fixing" me. And so I again was faced with the leap of faith.

I stepped out, and my feet touched a bridge. I saw nothing, but trusted with my eyes closed. For if I opened them, I would see the violent river rushing below me. After awhile, I found myself in a meadow, clean and peaceful, with no destructive river in sight, but rather a peaceful stream. Several times I was faced with such a chasm. But after awhile, I could see the bridge built by God's love for me.

When we trust in God, the first time, we have no reason, other than what we have been told, to believe the truth. Up to that point, we have usually tried to carry everything ourselves, and have found life too heavy, too wearying. Found ourselves to be too broken, too limited.

And yet we keep trying and falling, alone. There comes a time when we believe, no, most often only hope, that there is really something more. And we call out.

We call in faith, in hope, that someone will answer. That someone cares. That goodness is not something that we have imagined to exist.

We receive an answer. I remember, as a child, feeling how petty I was compared to God, and yet God loved me, wanted me when others did not. God hugged me when I was alone.

Once we experience God's love as fully as we can, faith becomes an assurance rather than a forlorn hope. We KNOW we will be heard, that we will be carried safely through the day, that all our needs will be met, that our fondest dreams will be surpassed.

We know this because God loves us in spite of ourselves, loves us exactly as we are, and we accept this gift and learn to dance.

"Come Let Us Walk in the Light of the Lord"
April 2005

My eyes cannot see. The darkness has wrapped them fully. The road behind me is filled with craters, holes such that if I turn around I would fall and not even my head would show should I find the will to stand up again. I know, because I barely made it through that maze of dangers. I know not what the road ahead holds, but I have no reason to think it any different.

No reason at all. But how can I travel forward? At least here, I am unhurt and alive. But what type of life is it? I cannot move my feet lest I lose track of where I am in relation to that hole behind me. Now, I know where it is. But if I move one foot, and then perhaps the other, how am I to keep track of where the hole is? How am I to know where the hole has gotten to in the darkness? There are only my fingers to count upon, to keep track of my footsteps, only my fingers to help me to remember.

Remember. Remember the times dancing in the daylight. Remember the times filled with the light of friendship. But those times are not here and now. Here and now holds only the holes, deep dangerous holes – and the darkness.

But how long can I live here, alone and without moving? How long can I even breathe here, not knowing for sure what is around me.

Promises have been made. My life is waiting for me elsewhere.

Promises, not only ones that I have made – but also ones that I have been given.

Lord, you have said that I only need to call upon you and you will have already answered. I call this day, this hour, this moment. I call upon you for help and safety.

And the darkness around me breaks. There, at the horizon, a light shines. There it expands, painting the sky shades of red and orange, dancing together. There, yellow comes up into the sky. Light begins to cover the landscape, painting it the colors of the rainbow, all colors except the color of darkness.

I look at the road in front of me. The holes are still there, but no longer the threatening danger of before. A move this way, and another that way, and I leave the holes behind. I move forward into my life once again. I dance forward into the light provided by my God.

I preached on Matthew 10:46-52 for my senior sermon in seminary, when I preached for all my professors and fellow students. I was lucky - my week was the one in which a camera crew was wandering around campus getting ready to make a promotional video for the seminary. So I got to preach to everybody with VERY bright lights shining in my face. I could only recognize the few people who sat in the first row. I had asked them to sit there on purpose, so that the cameras and the lights would not cause me to freeze. This September, I made it into story form from the outline.

Bartimaeus
September 2004 - first preached in 1992
from Mark 10:46-52

There is something special about the story of Bartimaeus in the Gospel of Mark. Unfortunately, we are not told much about his life. We don't know if he was born blind or had an accident. But we do know two things: we know what the author thought about him - he is called "Bartimaeus, son of Timaeus - which means "the honored son of the honored one." And we know what the people of his times thought of him - either he or his parents had sinned. Such blindness proved that God deservedly cursed Bartimaeus.

He was rejected by the townsfolk, sitting on the street corner, begging, living as an outcast whom the little boys tormented when they had nothing better to do. Living on other's charity, Bartimaeus knew that he did not deserve their scorn; he knew his parents did not either. But it was hard to hold onto his sense of self, to hold onto the knowledge that God loved him, when all disagreed with him.

And so, Bartimaeus sat, listening. Like many blind people, he heard much more clearly than those around him. Soon, rumors filled the town; rumors of a man called Jesus, a man who could heal, a man who taught about love, a man who cared. He heard those around him wondering just who this Jesus could be; Bartimaeus wondered and thought.

One day, commotion filled the town. He heard those claiming to be followers of Jesus, filled with confusion and speaking of their fear. They said that Jesus had said that he must suffer and die - and that those who followed him must die in order to live again. They were beginning to have second thoughts, thinking that perhaps the rich man who would not leave his riches was right. Bartimaeus listened, thinking, remembering the scriptures that had been read to him. As he sat there, praying, waiting, hoping that this Jesus would walk by his corner, warmth spread through his heart. He knew something that those who feared did not.

Suddenly, the noise around him grabbed his attention. Jesus was near! "Jesus, Son of David, have mercy on me!" he cried as loudly as he could. Those around him were scandalized. How dare this outcast even think of bothering the rabbi! And to call him by the title of Messiah, how dare he . . . "Jesus, son of David, have mercy on me!" Bartimaeus again cried even louder. The crowd began to get very angry, until Jesus heard the cry of faith and said, "Call him."

Some in the crowd told Bartimaeus what was said, and Bartimaeus jumped up, throwing off his cloak, and running for the first time in years toward that voice which was so filled with love. Running and falling at the feet of Christ, Bartimaeus was filled with hope. Jesus asked, "What do you want me to do for you?" Bartimaeus replied, "I want to see!" And then Christ said, "Your faith has healed you!" And Bartimaeus saw the feet of Christ in front of him, and he was filled with awe.

Jesus continued on his way along the road and into Jerusalem. Bartimaeus followed, following where those who were afraid could not go. He was not afraid, for he truly was loved.

Under a Bed - my story – February 2005

I found God under a bed when I was five. A neighbor lady had just told me that Jesus loved me and would "fix" me if I asked. I am eternally grateful that she spoke to me about her faith in God.

I found my mother's rosary beads while hiding under my mother's bed, trying to get away from further sexual abuse. I felt worthless and wasn't sure if anyone but the lady next door cared. My father might have, but it was my mother's job to care for the kids, and she cared for little but herself. I started talking to the figure of Jesus on the cross, and asked him to fix me because I hurt so much. Jesus did fix me - and I never experienced myself as alone ever again. Part of me sat in God's lap, experiencing God's arms holding me and hugging me close. Part of me felt wonderfully loved from that moment onward. Part of me sat bathed in light and knew what dancing was all about. The music of God's love surrounded me.

I don't remember much, except for the light, warmth and comfort, but I have touched God's presence almost constantly since that moment.

Now, I can call the experience a gift. As a minister, I have acknowledged my strong foundation in faith. At one point in my life, I stated that I would never give up my freedom in exchange for the past to have never happened, and I called that growth. Now I can say my whole life experience is a gift. Even today, when I ask for healing with the fullness of my faith, I still ask God to "fix" me, and I ask with the assurance of a five-year-old who knows that God will listen. When I ask God to heal those around me, I know something good will happen, and remarkable things occur.

That day sowed the seeds of trust, the seeds of self-acceptance, of openness to others; seeds that have since been watered and have burst forth into life. That part of me that touched God knew that I was not supposed to hate myself; that part of me taught me to love myself. Those seeds have led me to dance and to rejoice as the music of God's love fills my ears.

The five-year-old me only believed God could act on the inside, that God could reach down and heal me, that God could tell me whom to trust and what to do that would be the safest. The thirty-year-old me did NOT believe that God had anything to do with the outside world, for otherwise how could people have been so consistently nasty to me? I believed in "two kingdoms," the kingdom within where God ruled, and the kingdom without that evil ruled.

My life has truly been a dance of reaching out to those who reached out to me, and then feeling the fear, withdrawing, and reaching out again. It has been a dance of transformation.

When teaching high school in South Dakota, I attended the powwows first at the Mission School in Pine Ridge and then in Mission. I experienced dance as story for the first time in the movement of the warrior-dancers. I felt like a warrior each time I reached out, and then like a scared five-year-old each time I withdrew. The warrior won. The child has grown up and learned that fear is afraid of the light. And that there is no place that the light of God's love cannot reach.

The Warmth of the Sun - fiction - 1989

After twenty-six hours on the road, with many cups of coffee and only two donuts to eat, Matilda found herself with four speeding tickets for driving faster than she had ever driven before. She felt lost, out of control, fleeing from something, she forgot what - and then pain revived her memory, she saw flames engulf the house - and then she was on the road again, driving faster.

As a precaution, Matilda left the Interstate, to get away from the state police. She fled onto small country roads, curving around the mountain, her tires barely holding their own on the road. After two hours, a severe thunderstorm caught up with her, pounding the dry forest with hailstones. Some relief now that the outside world held some of the same turmoil she found within. In front, the lightning struck a fir tree and set it on fire, illuminating a curve she would else have missed; then the fire was put out by a torrent of rain, tears cascading down her face as if in reply, feeling the pain of the burning tree as if her own.

Vision blurred she still kept on, bump and off the road, still driving, though not as fast, now slowed, now stopped. Now crying, she felt a release of pain, sorrow, opening the door and into the rain, cold, tired, sleep.

The sun streamed through the windows of the hut, bright unceasing sunlight, a headache began to fill Matilda's head as soon as she opened her eyes. She was warm, under a blanket, her clothes drying next to the fire. Struggling, she put them back on, chagrined that a stranger had removed them. After success at that task, Matilda opened the door, the sunlight streamed in even more forcefully. As if trying to punish herself, she ventured outside into the brightness.

There, a short bald man tended to a garden, healing the damage done by the violence of the storm. He was having trouble setting some pole beans back to rights, so Matilda decided to pay back his kindness and help. She slipped in the mud and broke the pole he had been working with. "Klutz, klutz", she kept saying to herself, "klutz, klutz", as if by saying it she was condemning herself.

But the man's laughter knocked the word out of her mind. Confusion as to where she was and what she was doing filled her. She looked up and a man was laughing at her. At her! But then she supposed she did look funny covered with mud and goo.

She tried to accept the man's help getting up, but they both ended up down instead. "My wife's gonna wonder what we've been up to," he said.

Relief crept into her pain; at least the man hadn't undressed her, she thought. Although why would she care with her husband dead, burned to death in a fire started by their daughter playing with matches, the very matches Matilda had left on the table. He had died saving all the kids. Kids that Matilda couldn't look at as they all looked like him, blue eyes, wide smile...Kids she'd left at her parents in her flight from what life held out to her.

Kids, the man was talking about kids now. He'd had some, they'd died though, he was sorry, but he'd go on living, life was worth the effort. Hogwash.

Well, maybe not. The warm sun was no longer paining her eyes, but rather warming her blood, frozen by her flight. The hut was in a clearing, a stream wandered by, a small orchard, and a mountain vista in the distance. A postcard almost, except it was real.

This wasn't the first time Matilda had reacted to pain by flight. She'd run away when her brother had died, too.

The pain was very similar, except this time, she felt she really did deserve the blame. But then, what could she do to bring her love back...except love those who had his eyes, his smile, and his heart.

Her son had tried to blame himself, but Matilda wouldn't listen. Although he had been baby sitting, she was the one who left the matches. But even so, if he blamed himself the way she blamed herself...Matthew, why did you have to die!

Tears, sorrow. "Don't hold on and out it flows, "the man whispered as he held her as she cried. "If you hold onto it, it freezes your ability to love, to care, to heal others." Matilda had told her story in her sleep, and the man had listened.

"I thought I caused my kids' death," he began. "But, we can't keep blaming ourselves even if we did do wrong. Guilt keeps life out, self-pity kills more than guns ever do," he said slowly.

She listened to his story, feeling the echoes of his pain. When he got to his wife's part, blaming herself, too, Matilda began to think of her son again.

"Love calls us back to life," the man said. And Matilda felt love calling. She felt her son's pain across the distance, a mother's love binding her to him. She couldn't go to him yet, but after awhile she would. After dealing with her own pain and sorrow, she would be better equipped to help him out of his own darkness. Matt Junior wasn't going to be stuck in guilt, not if his mom could help it.

Lighted by Faith - meditation - 2005

It is hard to imagine what life would be like without the presence of faith to light the dark corners. Fear would have a greater place within my heart. Fear is still present; it hides in the corner until I try to do something difficult, something that works against those who caused my abusive childhood. Then fear does its best to tell me how dangerous such an undertaking is. Fear seeks to cause me to protect myself, to believe that protecting myself to be the highest goal that there is.

But self-protection is not the highest goal. It is an important goal, surely. We don't walk the dark city streets at night without looking around us, seeking as much safety as possible. Some streets we avoid even in the daylight without someone to walk with us. Fear does serve its purpose in preventing us from doing many a silly thing. But we should not let it chain us to our houses with the shades drawn so that no light can get in, for it is light that gives us life. Nor can we bar our hearts if we wish to live. Fear should not be allowed to dictate to us what we should do.

Our faith is a far better rule to follow. Faith becomes a beacon in the darkness of our fears. I can't imagine what life would be like without my encounter with God under the bed. I probably never would have gotten out from under the bed. I know I never would have written this book. I have done many things that without the light of faith I never could have accomplished.

I still get stuck sometimes. And Jesus stands before me, asking me if I want to be healed. Sometimes I say no, I like hiding. The darkness is much more comfortable than forgiving people who have hurt me once again. The darkness is much more comfortable than reaching out again, only to be hurt again. For it is in reaching out that we get hurt.

But it is in reaching out that we get healed, that the pain filling our heart lessens through the touch of the light of those who care about us. It is in leaving the darkness behind that we learn more about life. It is in leaving fear behind that the music fills our hearts again and we begin to dance to the music of life.

Eventually, I get bored of the darkness and accept the gift that is offered to me. And the light of God's love makes the darkness that had filled my life disappear. And I begin again on the road to greater love and wholeness. I begin once more to dance.

Seeds of Trust - 1989

Silence surrounding the child
echo less vacuum, desert dry world
frozen, no brightness.
Sitting, eyes closed, mind shut
speaking within to One who listens.

Listening herself, for love which comes
surrounds, makes light
teaching integrity
wholeness.

Outside - chaos, pain, owned guilt
used object
discarded.
Inside peace, warmth, forgiveness
beloved being
treasured.

Seeds of trust
planted, grow
watered in spite of wounds
by wounds healing.

Universe transforming
slowly unfolding
newness surprising
yet always was there
smothered by hate.

Seeds of self
hidden grow
watered by moments of oneness
being of people.

Universe transforming
rapidly growing
lightness surprising
yet new, yet more
self hidden
recovered.

Seeds of openness
planted grow
watered in spite of pain
by pain.

Universe transforming
rainbows bursting
enlightening others
yet always remembering
what was, might still have been.

Seeds of life
unfolding grow
watered by sharing, giving,
dancing duets.

Surprised by self
affirmed by others
standing, speaking, shouting.
Strength, uniqueness echoed back

by a world rain bowed with wonder
filled with beings clothed in uniqueness
filled with a future dreams could not tell.
Dancing alone, yet encircled
Dancing together yet as one.
Dancing with the ones
who listen.

April 2005

Faith allows us to dance in the darkness as it whispers to us where the obstacles are that may trip us up. Faith lends us ears to hear the words of encouragement sent by God from the lips of strangers and friends. Faith opens our eyes to whatever light there may be in whatever the darkness is that may surround us. It is a tremendous gift.

My Life's Blessing - my story - January 2006

I have, at times, felt sorry for myself. I have been quite angry with God. I've even refused to speak or even "look at" God. But since that time at five-years-old under the bed, I have NEVER doubted God's existence.

Nor have I ever doubted God's love. I have doubted God's promise to care for me and help me, not because I doubted God's power to do so, but because I doubted my own worthiness of that care and help. If I truly deserved it, would not my parents have given me some as well?

My father, having given my mother the responsibility to care for the children as he provided for us all, does not deserve the same indictment as my mother. At some point, scholarship told me that we model our images of God on our parents. My Dad was the one I picked for such conscious modeling. And so I held that watchmaker image of God, the God who set everything in motion as if a watchmaker. Once motion began, that God took no responsibility for how things turned out; it was solely up to us people.

I experienced a major split between my conscious experience of God and my unconscious one; fortunately, my unconscious image of a loving, caring and active God is the real one. That active God is the God that I know and love in return, the one who I serve as an ordained minister of word and sacrament.

My sure knowledge of God's existence is why I am alive to write this book. And that is my life's blessing that I share.

Movement Two - As it Sometimes Grows Dark

April 2005

We often have a "dark night of the soul," when we aren't sure what life is all about, when the foundations of our life crumble into nothingness and we wonder if there is anything solid at all that we can stand upon. The faith that we have built up to that point is what sustains us as we travel through the darkness. The power of God's love gives us the strength to make it to the other side. And when we need them, God sends "angels", messengers, to help us, whether they be human, canine, or an event or actual spiritual beings - the sun shining on a summer's morning, a robin when we doubt spring will ever come, a sense of presence when we are being driven crazy by our isolation – all these God can and does use to help light our way in the darkness.

As it Sometimes Grows Dark - my story - 1989

Things happen to us at times with which we cannot cope - and so we "create" a world in which to live that we can handle. This happens to those of us growing up in an alcoholic environment. The denial gives us the strength to grow up, but after awhile that denial limits who we can become, as much of our resources go to keeping the secret. The denial limits how we deal with people as it masks the pain, fear and anger. Even though denied, the pain, fear and anger control how we see the world. Ways of coping that allowed us to live and survive when we were children chain and control us as we live as adults.

I created a fantasy world, a world that I called "real" and lived therein; the truth of my life was too painful to grasp. In my fantasy, I had the "bestest" daddy and the "bestest" mommy, although my mommy was always sick and couldn't love me the way she wanted to; add three kids and you have the very "bestest" family in the whole world. And I believed it as hard as I could because that was what my mommy was always telling me was true; and you should always believe your mommy because mommies know best. And I really believed it because none of it was true.

I never would have believed anyone could hide from himself or herself anything of the nature I locked deep within. My memory trained itself to forget rather than to remember. But I have learned there are many people who have experienced this. With a catalyst or trigger, such as a death, at the right age, we begin to heal from the ravages of the pain life has dealt out to us. I have met many women like myself who "forgot" the sexual abuse that occurred in their childhoods. Many women like myself who wondered if they were crazy as terrors and pieces of memories began to surface; who finally stopped feeling guilt and blame for what had happened as if they, at three, four or five, could have prevented an adult from doing what he or she had wanted to do; who finally start to learn to love the person God created them to be. I found it hard to remember when most of my family remembered nothing of this. Without my sister's support and memory that verified some of my own, I would have decided I was crazy.

When my mother had a stroke, I flew in from South Dakota to visit her in the hospital in New Jersey. My father, sister and brother were visiting her hospital room at the same time. I was holding my mother's hand when my father mentioned something about my return to my teaching job in South Dakota. At this point, my mother used great effort to push me away and refused to say good-bye to me when I left. My father comforted me as I walked out into the hall. The next day she died, and so I returned. Later, neither my father nor my brother remembered my mother pushing me away. My sister did. My sister remembered many other things.

Soon after, the volcano inside me began to steam, to smoke, sputter, and finally erupt - my mother's death was the catalyst of my freedom, freedom from chains forged of terror and pain which had bound my soul since I was five years old. Through counseling and the support of newfound friends, I was able to contain the phases of this eruption, to deal with the truth that forced itself back into my mind, demanding my attention.

While still a child, I could not have survived the pain, anger, terror, and aloneness that then engulfed who I was, now all of it emerging in a kaleidoscope of ragged memories, fragments as damaging as shrapnel from a land mine. Emotions stuffed into forgetfulness as a child, flowing out, demanding attention, with such overwhelming force I was sure I must be insane, at least until I met others dealing with the same type of experiences. We were not going insane, but rather we were instead becoming sane and healthy. As an adult, choosing to remember, to enter the darkness of the past, I not only survived but also stepped into freedom, a world peopled with wonders I could not have imagined - peopled with those who have become my friends.

I am awed when I realize what it feels like to be able to actually like myself, when I imagine what it might be like to love myself someday - after having been taught to hate myself, to especially hate my body because owning a body made me vulnerable and able to be victimized. I am left speechless when I contemplate the love my God showers upon me. I am overwhelmed when I try to accept God's gift of friends and loved ones who want me, want me to be a part of their lives, as I want them in mine.

This "travelogue" is difficult to write. I find myself rereading what I have written over the last six years. Pieces of what I have written hit hard, the pain echoes within me again, though with a fraction of the force it once had.

I remember four years ago when it really started rolling out - I could not handle full time work. After a counseling session, even if it was a morning session, I spent the remainder of the day asleep, dealing with the fragments of myself was difficult work. I just let the pent-up, once-denied pain flow out, sometimes I could only just roll around on my bed as it hurt so much. Much of this pain was also birth pangs as life began flowing into me. Some weeks I could not work at all as a substitute teacher, other weeks I managed as much as 3 days. It all depended upon the ebb and flow of pain and healing released from my inner, hidden self.

I had truly turned myself off. I had forgotten everything I could, practically everything that had happened before I went to college. I participated in life as though it were a television show with the sound turned off, a black and white set, hidden in the other corner of the room, the lights turned low so as to allow the dim set to be seen. I tried hard to figure out what was going on, but I couldn't get close enough. I did not realize how lonely I was because I didn't know anything else existed. My life was controlled by my past.

My mother had been an alcoholic. Her disease, while "under the influence", resulted in her doing things she would have cringed at the thought of when sober. And she drank more, mixed with tranquilizers, other drugs, in her attempt to run from her pain, to find oblivion. She controlled the entire family in an attempt to feel in control of her out-of-control life. My life, the lives of my whole family, revolved around her guilt, her pain. Only her pain was allowed to be real, ours was unimportant, make-believe, denied.

Later, I discovered much of the anger I felt was really my mother's anger. There was very little in the way of boundaries between my mother and myself. Her emotions bled over into mine. One day, during the third year of counseling, I felt my mother's anger leave me. And the next time I met with my counselor, she felt something different. Eventually, she decided that what was different was that she no longer felt fear of me. Without my mother's anger filling me, the amount of anger that I kept tied up inside myself diminished. I began to lose my own fear of myself. And I began to learn anger is not something to be feared, but rather a tool that tells us something is wrong, that needs to be fixed. I learned anger itself could be used as a fuel for growth, which is NOT something that my mother ever learned.

As a child, I preferred my make-believe world to the knowledge that my mother was destroying herself. It really didn't matter to me then what she did to me - I thought I deserved anything and everything bad that might happen to me. By blaming myself, I managed to create the illusion that something in my life was under my control.

My mother's alcoholism destroyed her capacity to think, to feel, and to live. The way she created the illusion that she was somehow in control of at least part of her life was to control someone else, to abuse and hurt. My mother slowly destroyed what was left of her ability to love anyone, especially herself. And so she died.

Yet I live. I found Jesus and was "fixed" by him when I was five years old. I lived on the inside and shut out what happened to my body. I turned the sound off in my life, turned off my emotions until I was old enough to make sense of them. When I was strong enough and mature enough to withstand the furies, my journey back into the darkness began, a journey that would bring me out again and into a world filled with so much light and love that I could not have imagined it.

At first, the pieces I found made no sense. Pieces of one day took a year and a half to remember - a day that took away my ability to speak, to trust - for a while. I lived as if in a room alone, with the hurtful world closed out. And I decided to open the door to let love in. When I had not the strength, the courage, my Lord Jesus carried me, healed me so I could walk, run, soon to dance.

Profound change has occurred in my life. The sound turned on in a room used to quiet - deafness threatening from the sudden loudness, color that infused life into the darkness overwhelmed my senses with details, and suddenly, no more television show, but real life surrounded me, grabbed me, pulled me, and then I no longer knew who "me" was - at least until I got used to the new level of life within and around me. New information overwhelmed me as parts long dead came alive; the newly alive parts of me felt as would an arm or a leg having "fallen asleep" coming alive again, with the "pins and needles" multiplied a thousand-fold. At times, I felt as if I were flying upside down in a small plane through thunderstorms and with no one piloting the plane, only my faith in Jesus Christ.

Peace has come. I rejoice in intimacy and closeness, I dance with friends. I still hide at times when something in the present comes too close to something in my past, I still find myself surprised to discover new pieces of myself.

I find myself reading with echoes of pain the words I wrote as I traveled into the darkened past, and feel thankful I have finally come out on the other side of the tunnel. A tunnel so dark I just knew I would get lost and never see light again, but that wasn't true either, and here I am, ready to share my life with you. I rejoice in the rainbow I now see when I look through these tears I have cried.

Reprise - January 2006

And again, my own words remind me of where I have traveled in this journey. The journey of this past year has seemed difficult, but the reminder of where I have been makes those mountains just traveled seem like molehills. I see the fear that still existed in the words that I wrote twenty years ago, fear of the pain that comes with just being alive, for I had so much of that pain stuck inside me. But many of those body memories filled with fear have been slowly chased out as yoga has taught me to live in my body. Light and fear do not co-exist well. Now "just being alive" fills me with anticipation, not fear. Being alive is the most wonderful thing I can imagine.

Vision - prose poem - 1989

Today, Lord, I seek a vision. I seek a reason, a meaning. I see men around me building castles in the sand, only to see their handiwork washed away at the next tide. I see refuse brought in by the tide: broken bottles, broken boats, broken shells, broken dreams.

Today, Lord I seek a vision. I hear the pounding of the surf, wearing away the beach, encroaching on homes of men until those homes come crashing down as victims of time. I hear the slow remorseless beat of the sea as it steals someone else's dreams and visions. I hear the disorder, the tumult of sea gulls, I see them diving, fighting, crashing, with only the sea as the winner.

I have followed your words, Lord. I have striven and studied, but I am as an empty shell, an empty boat upon the sea, sent hither and yon at the mercy of the wind - touching no one, touched by no one. Lord, what is it that I lack? Everything I see falls apart at my touch. Lord, please send a vision to uphold my faith.

Silence answered me. The gulls and sunbathers had left me alone with the sea as the sun had set. I still walked along the beach, searching for the vision I knew I would find. Silence was broken, and I was greatly annoyed, as I thought I had almost found an answer in the moonlight shining upon my face. Annoyed at the interruption, annoyed at the people who were gathering near to celebrate.

Celebrate? Celebrate the destruction growing in our world; celebrate the pain in the faces around us?

I looked at those people with anger, and saw the light of God in their hearts.

Grudgingly, I joined the celebration. Several people had come to the beach to meditate and pray in thanksgiving. One of their number had been cured of a horrible disease, another continued to feel great pain, but smiled in hope. I joined hands with them and prayed, and in their faces, shining with Your Love, Lord, I found my vision.

As It Sometimes Grows Dark - meditation -1989

Lord, I am lost. I act in the freedom of the knowledge of your love for me as I have been created to be by your infinite wisdom. I act out of the love for humanity which you have placed within me, that love that thirsts to enfold all brokenness with healing, to enfold all loneliness with comfort; that love that thirsts to lead all who will follow into the growth of truth. Yet many laugh, throw scorn and disdain, hiding behind smug sophistication. They push all those who will not follow their lead into a quicksand of condemnation and lies.

I will not absolve them from ignoring the poor, of oppressing and controlling those without the power to reply. Absolution belongs to your domain, my Lord. Self-righteous sophistication - looking down on your creation as a thing to be used, claiming knowledge without purpose or humility, morality without a base in the paradox of the cross - these do not speak of your kingdom. And it is your kingdom for which I seek, to which I dedicate myself, your kingdom for which I risk when I stand and speak the truths you have burned within my heart and soul.

It is to give humanity life that you died; it is the demanding nature of your love, which caused you to sacrifice yourself. Truth is never something that is dead, but rather it is something that lives and breathes the life of resurrection and love; it is singing with gladness and joy, songs speaking of the transformation which your love has built into our lives. Truth does not cause suffocation, but rather pulls us out of the mire, makes us clean and fills us with newness.

"Out of my distress I called on the Lord..."[1] and I am set free. My Lord, you are my refuge in whom I place my confidence. Yes, and you send me your spirit which fills my being, she nurtures me with your fire of love, she translates your truth into words which I can hear and understand. And so a book is filled with life, words become scripture that send terror into the hearts of those hoping for a spiritless life, fear into those who will not let go of their privilege of acceptance by the crowds for the risk of following your truth.

They do not listen, they hide their ears, and yet your words follow them.

"Therefore, I tell you, the kingdom of God will be taken away from you and given to a nation producing the fruits of it."[2]

Where is their fruit? I look upon the poverty-filled cities, I look upon the slagheaps littering your creation, and I look into pain-filled eyes of children, of starving mothers nursing... And yet, I try...to love those who throw condemnation at me, for they too are created and loved by you. For this I need your grace. Perhaps one of these will come into your kingdom because I obeyed your command to love.

Perhaps...rejected by the builders who control the present world, perhaps I will become a part of the foundation of your kingdom. For my fondest wish is to help you heal your creation, to soothe the pain in the child's eyes, to feed the starving mothers so that they, too, can feed your children.

---

[1] From Psalm 130
[2] Matthew 21:43

Lord, "I thank you that you have answered me and have become my salvation."[3] Without you, I am nothing, I am dead, and I am truly lost. With you, my Lord, I can face the world, I am lost for but the moment in which I lose sight of you; but you always turn me around and show me your presence in my life. Be with me and inspire me with your truth, love and wisdom. Fill me with your Holy Spirit so that she may guide me to your will and aid as
you teach me to love.

---

[3] Psalm 118:21

Of a Labyrinth Freed   - 1989

Lost in a Labyrinth of tears
Blinded by Blackness, deaf in a void
peopled by screams stilled by timelessness
memories of light dimmed
by faithless works
of those who destroy life for sport.

I am lost, but not forsaken
For as I let go of my chains
another, greater than myself, breaks them.
I cry, years of tears, of pain a river.
Seeds of life now watered sprout.
Tears are real, perhaps to be feared,
but never to be feared is Thy love

Lost, wishing to be found,
to loose these chains of tears,
I cannot find a way
tripping forever, burdened by anger
molding hatred to frozen tears
uncried, ignored in solitary stillness.

And so I shall continue to trust as told.
I shall hope against logic as I listen,
hope as I have since I began my search,
search for people, to trust-
to love with the frozen river of love
still inside, which flows from my Lord to me, and
hopefully some day, flowing freely
to the world around me.

But pain, loneliness chill my heart.

Yes, my Lord felt such himself on a cross,
for to love man is to love imperfection,
limited, often broken, hate filled, fearful beings,
But with love-all share in His Life.

And wishing a share of life, of joy,
I follow my Lord's promise,
I shall allow my river to thaw
from the fire of faith gifted to me,
send my river to nourish the hungry
the parched and broken
as my Lord commands me,
Someday to dance in joy,
as I share the bountiful gifts of
my Lord, my God.

As I Was Taught - my story - January 2006

My mother taught me that anger was when you threw martini glasses at your five-year-old daughter. The church I grew up in taught me that anger was a great sin, one that must be confessed to God. And so anger was something that I stuffed, that I used much of who I was to still and control. Fear I would overcome, it was not an invincible enemy, but anger was.

Compared to now, I was about 4 percent alive - at most. I was frozen with emotions I did not dare to feel; many events were forgotten in order to maintain my sanity, part of me was broken off. I wasn't really sure I had a body, and if I did, I certainly did not want to live in it.

But those who have been my counselors have taught me that anger is a sign that something is wrong; it is a sign that there is something that we need to address before the pressure cooker of our hearts blow up. After much re-learning, I am no longer afraid of anger. I now let myself feel anger and deal with it appropriately; I get angry now when you cut me off in traffic, but I leave the road rage to someone else. I take good care of my pressure cooker. My heart is now free.

From out of the Depths - March 1990
Psalm 130 - Lectionary Stuff

Lost in a Labyrinth of tears
Deep in a well of blackness blinded
memories of light dimmed, almost gone,
hidden by sin -
of those who destroy for sport
hidden by faithless works - mine own.

Lost, wishing to be found
to loose these chains of tears
I cannot find a way
tripping, burdened by anger
ignored in solitary stillness.

Lost in the night
waiting for sunrise
waiting for the fruits of promise
waiting for the forgiveness of my Lord
A night the light will fill
with colors painting the sky with life.

Forgiveness finds, enfolds me
I cry -
Seeds of life now watered sprout
rainbows fill a forgiven heart
dancing in worship to an awesome God.

On Becoming a Soft Shell Crab – meditation – April, 2005

My pastor once used an analogy that really made an impact on me. As I was a seminary student at the time, I listened closely. I felt I could use all the wisdom I could find. He spoke of the life of a soft shell crab. At first, the crab lives in safety, in a hard shell. But the crab grows, while the shell doesn't. If the crab stays in the shell, it smothers and dies. Instead, it leaves its shell behind and spends a significant period of time as a soft shell crab, one whose life is filled with vulnerability, in which almost everything could act as a predator. The crab continues to experience life, but only at the cost of extreme vulnerability.

This story resonated with me, for that is what I had done. I have left the safety of my imagined world, and come out into a sea of chaos, a place in which, at first, I had no idea who was foe and who was friend. When I began to remember and deal with my childhood, the shell I was living in was so hard and tight around me that I could not have imagined the life that flowed about me every day. I held on tightly to God, and ignored everything else as much as I could.

The period of intense remembering, when many things triggered more memories, was a time filled with vulnerability. When I began, I spoke with my eyes closed – to God, not to my counselor. And as I healed, a safer, larger shell grew around me. This cycle repeated several times as I continued to grow. Eventually, it became hard to decide to leave my perceived place of safety, as the place in which I was living became a more comfortable place in which to live.

Fortunately, by the time I heard this analogy, I was no longer experiencing chaos of hurricane force. But I still had more places to heal; I still had to make the decision to leave my safe, hardened shell and venture into life. I kept discovering that my then-current shell was insufficient to hold the number of people I was allowing into my heart. The act of writing this book has been another soft shell crab experience, one also filled with transformation and healing. I wrote one version for me and then this one to share with you.

To some extent, we are all challenged to make this decision at one time or another, and to continue our own process of transformation. Growth and transformation do not occur without risk, and when one moves into risk nothing is ever really sure. In the darkness, dangers do lurk.

But God heals the new hurts and pain just as easily as the old ones. I admit I found it harder to present the new hurts to God for healing, as those hurts occurred while I was the soft shell crab being challenged to take risks by my faith. At these times, God then reminds me of the quality of my life before the chaos moved into it, before I had ever started to heal. Then I realize that the change that results is worth taking the risk. That doesn't mean I like the soft shell crab experience, just that I realize that it is necessary to experience the fullness of life.

We don't really live in shells, so what is it that forms our protective armor? We become accustomed to the way we do things. Our system of organizing reality becomes comfortable and solid. It saves us from allowing the unfamiliar into our lives; it allows us to ignore the existence of that which does not fit. Our reality system allows us to make decisions without even thinking about them or wondering what the consequences of our decisions might be. Our system allows us to exclude those whose experience of reality is different than ours.

As a teacher, I learned that people's brains really are wired differently. I needed to express what I was trying to teach in different ways if I wanted as many students as possible to understand what I was saying. That is one reason why this book expresses the truth of my life in different literary forms. The other reason is that I NEED the poetry and story to more fully express myself.

Churches often oppose that which would call them into growth by saying "we've never done it that way before." My favorite instance of this came when my previous congregation told me this in the fourth year I was their pastor - and I was suggesting that we do something the way we had done whatever it was for the previous three years. But this was after September 11, 2001, and we were a congregation only 140 miles from New York City. That which was different was scarier that year. "We've never done it that way before" is an attitude that fears that which is new; it is an attitude that fears that which challenges. Nothing can stay the same and experience life at its fullest and at its most faith filled, not even churches. If we don't use our faith, its strength diminishes.

Individually, we have our armor, old habits and ways of doing things that give us an excuse not to grow. Perhaps, we have problems forgiving. Perhaps, we are afraid of allowing ourselves to care, as we have been hurt in the past. I often state in sermons that it is easy to tell in an end of life care center who it was who allowed love into their lives, and who it was who shut their hearts down, armored in steel lest someone or something come to mean

44

something to them that could cause hurt. This second group exudes brittleness and makes life difficult for those who give care. The first group brings joy into the lives of the caregivers.

We all face the decision made by the hard shell crab: to take a risk that really could result in injury and allow transformation and growth to expand our experience of life, or to stay in the shell, and slowly suffocate. When we allow fear to control our choice rather than faith, our choice becomes as limited as our lives. It is difficult to choose the life of a soft shell crab, because it does hold the risk of pain. But there is also pain involved in staying in the shell. Reaching out in faith and putting your trust in God makes that choice possible. Our whole world is faced with the choice of the crab at this point in time. Each individual's decision helps create the decision made by the world.

Someone Told Her - fiction - 1989

Someone told her love was having a bottle of wine at a candlelit dinner. And so she married the owner of a vineyard. But she discovered that good wine did not make love. Her man cared more for his vines than he did for her. Soon she had nightmares of being consumed by giant grapes as she found her husband spending more and more time nurturing his vines.

Then she met the vineyard's accountant, with his columns of figures that grew into mountainous piles - especially in this man's bank account. The accountant bought her what the vineyard owner was too busy to buy: furs and cars and a soft bed to lie upon. She left the vineyard owner to his vines and followed the accountant.

But she soon found the accountant and his numbers sterile, passionless. She ran away, still looking for life, and found herself standing in a zoo. The lion was so kingly, but the oxen were strong, even the grizzly bear seemed, for a moment, enticing. She tried all she could think of, until she finally found herself alone, with only an ass.

And so, at last, she cried. She could not find love however hard she tried. A shadow fell over her, but she did not notice. The zookeeper had finished his rounds. He was ugly and unkempt. She never would have noticed him had he not noticed her tears.

"Poor lady, I have nothing to give you but my heart. All I receive from tending these animals is their love-but I can share that with you," he said as he knelt before her, unable to bear her suffering.

She looked up and saw something she had never seen before, a stream of love flowing out of someone's eyes and into her heart. Her own love began to flow out of

46

where she had hidden it, and met his. The two streams merged, making a river of love. She did not notice his ragged clothes; she did not miss the wine and jewels. Her heart was no longer damned. And soon they began to dance together.

Darkness Dissolving - my story - April 2005

Darkness does not stay when we reach toward the light. Yes, the darkest part of my healing journey took several years, but the darkness wasn't triumphant during that time or during my childhood. God always sent someone – or some dog – to help guide me and accompany me.

When I started remembering the content of my childhood, that darkness in which part of me had always lived became the darkness in which almost all of me lived. The only part of me really conscious of the light was that which still sat on God's lap. That five-year-old's faith is what gave me the courage to start my journey.

I lived with my father at this time. His support during these years made up in part for the neglect of my childhood when he followed the cultural rules and put his wife in complete charge of his children. I find reassurance in the thought that those rules are no longer iron clad and unchallenged. My childhood might have gone quite differently if custody of children in a divorce had not gone automatically to the mother. My father neglected me when I was a child, but gave much support while I was healing as an adult. He grew and accepted the challenge of transformation as well.

Darkness dissolves when light comes into the world.

Movement Three - Hope

November 2004

This movement is about hope, especially the hope that was given to me by all God's people who interacted with me during the course of my growth. God sent many people into my life to help me, to reach out and touch me, to be God's presence in my life, to show me the path of transformation.

Touching Spirit - my story - February 2005

When my dog Spirit came into my life, she had no idea what being petted was all about. She jumped into my lap because my older dog, Dewey, taught her that that was what dogs should do in our household. When I petted her, she bristled. Her hair felt as if I was petting a porcupine against the grain. My hand tingled with negative energy.

Spirit came from a shelter just as Dewey did. She'd been caught running around loose, eating from people's garbage cans. (Would you believe that I couldn't train her to leave my garbage can alone? If I leave food on the table on a plate, she leaves it alone, even if I have finished with it. But if I put it in the garbage can, I have obviously relinquished title to the food - and it is HERS!) Her previous owner had taught her that touch felt BAD - and so she bristled.

But this touch thing intrigued her. There was something about it that felt GOOD. I continued to pet her, and she kept being intrigued, wondering just what it was that felt good about it. She wanted more of it. She started lying right next to Dewey in Dewey's dog bed. Dewey felt insulted, but then soon he decided he liked having someone lying next to him. It felt almost as good as being petted.

Spirit got her name from the adult Bible study class. I brought her in to be introduced, attached to Dewey on the same lead. Dewey said "Friends! Friends, who will pet me. Friends who will pet me NOW!" as he ran over to the members of the class.

Spirit, meanwhile, was saying, "People? How can I trust people . . ." as Dewey dragged her behind him. Eventually, Spirit no longer had to be dragged over to a member of the congregation. She started going up to them on her own. She started asking, as did Dewey, to be petted. She started EXPECTING the congregation to pet her.

She started jumping into my lap because she wanted to, and not just because Dewey told her that that was what dogs do. The bristling stopped. Now she demands being petted as her due as the dog in charge of security. She demands petting from everyone whom she deems to be part of her pack. She is now as much of a wagtail dog as Dewey.

I had similar experience with being touched. Childhood had taught me that touching did not feel good. But in my adult life, I found friends whom I trusted whose touch gave me a different experience; the healing hands of chiropractors also helped redefined what touch was all about. After a time, I began to feel the same intrigue that Spirit felt. Something about being hugged actually felt good.

Finally, someone touched me - and all that I felt from it was "good touch." It was then that I realized that why I hadn't been into being touched and hugged was because it had felt bad. The distrust that had frozen in my heart had melted. And touch felt GOOD. The painful touching that I had received had lost its power. The lesson that no one could be trusted also lost its power and was replaced with a different lesson, that people can be the arms of God and give hugs
almost as good God does.

Hope - meditation - 1989

Hope - a little magic word that can transform one's world from black to rainbow. Without it, no one would embark upon a spiritual journey of healing, for what would be the use?

Hope gives us little bits of Joy to spice our life. Every now and then in our journey, we experience that special moment in which we know, for a moment, what life is all about. We feel at one with the world around us, at one with God. Sometimes, it is the unspoken promise of these moments that gives us the courage to continue to live.

Joy teaches us many things that make life worth living. With joy we feel the loosening of our chains of pain, we learn to dance anyplace and everyplace, unceasingly in joyous gratitude, in celebration of the life that fills us to bursting.

Yet, after awhile, the reality of still being human returns, and the burning coals that we have been dancing on begin to sting a bit. Our joy falters, stumbles, our previous method of coping with life beckons like an old pair of shoes after a day spent in stiff, shiny, new ones.

But hope holds our hand when we lose our footing, and faith sends us searching anew for joy. This is itself a dance, with repeating movements, themes; and after awhile, if we keep moving on, the moments of joy come more often.

We truly choose how we will live our lives. A stream of love flows swiftly through the clearing, yet many too afraid to drink of the stream die of thirst. The grain grows majestically throughout, yet pathetic stick figures surround us. We choose whether to accept the love offered to us; to see truth and grow or to see darkness and despair;

whether to allow our pain to grow into love within us. The greatest gift of love is joy. Joy does not demand a full stomach, but rather a full heart. Joy blesses pain that has been washed in love. Joy quiets despair and nourishes hope. Joy teaches us how to use anger to create rather than to destroy.

Joy hungers to share with others, to love, to flow through us to others hungry for love, for joy - to heal whatever pain surrounds it. Joy, faith, hope - all restore our confidence as we traverse our own particular valleys. We are not alone; we are never alone once we accept the gift of love.

These two poems speak of hope and dancing, two things that go very well together.

Hopscotch Hope - 1989

The child runs upstairs crying
searches for hugs of healing
No luck.
The child runs downstairs crying
out the door into the park.

Pain twists her face
a wet rag wrung with loneliness.
Hoping for someone,
anyone to chase the pain,
the fears, the clouds away.

Tripping, she falls beneath a tree
The soul cries out in shame
for someone
anyone to answer, to care
to make safe the world
once more.

Someone's puppy dog whines
licks a wet, uplifted face.
The tears taste good,
puppy thinks
and soon all tears are gone.

The pain not gone, quite,
but fears move onto
another lonely day.
For now a friend
brings the storm to end
the broken heart will mend.

The child skips around the pond
New friend following gamely
For someone
answered a child's prayer
and sent gleaming hope.

Dancing Magic - 1989

The magic tiptoes now
among the faith-filled few.
Touching, leaping, touching again
those sitting within the pew.

The magic walks firmly
through the golden voices.
And though a note sounds ill,
still magic touches all.

Now skipping along
the path at dawn
the sunrise service
it blesses twice

Now skipping through
this afternoon
the self-help group
it blesses thrice

Dancing and waltzing and healing pain
The magic touches all who call
for help, for hope.
The magic touches,
a person changes
a lantern of hope
a light of joy

a strife-filled world
a pain-filled soul
a darkened mind
a forgotten child
now the light of hope
the light of grace
the light of love.

The magic touches
wordlessly, prayerfully,
all who call
in hope, in faith,
in love.

Dancing Upon the Hilltop - prose poem - 1989

In the distance stands a lonely hill. Upon it a sole tree reaches only so far, it does not touch the sky, the swirling clouds above way beyond its reach.

I feel like the smallest leaf on that tree. Insignificant, attached to a church which doesn't quite make it in this world; cut off from the rest of humanity which doesn't care, doesn't care that it will not touch the sky, dreaming only of that which it can pile up for posterity.

Posterity-save for "future generations." To take and take from the earth and its people wealth to such an extent that future generations are in doubt. But for what else is life?

The whirling wind creates a dust devil in the road between the hill and myself. Quickly made and then dissolved to nothing. So will a man's life and the wealth he creates for his posterity be dust. To dust all does return in this world.

"In this world", perhaps that's my problem. I search for my answers in this world. I should walk around with my eyes upon the clouds, not upon the earth that others profane with their posterity. But then, do I see the widows and their children, the homeless, the victims of disease whom my Lord has commanded me to love if I look always upward to the clouds?

But more importantly, do I see the healing hand of my Lord at work as the lame learn to dance and the deaf learn to sing? Or do I see even the paradox of the terminally ill at peace with both life and death, of the flowers growing amidst rubble and decay?

58

If I am to look not toward the clouds or to the earth, then where am I to look? If I look within I see only my own lostness, my own hatreds, my own brokenness and inability to act as I should. If I look into the eye of my brother, I find nothing more than a mirror of myself.

The world around me holds no answer. Yes, the birds trill in the trees, but there is no thrill from within me. The land around is beautiful, but that too will turn to dust as soon as no rain falls, or winter's cold enthralls it. The wind will endlessly wear away that far hill, for nothing in this world is permanent.

But my Lord's promise is permanent. My faith wavers as at moments such as this, but my cries are always answered, as I know they will be answered at this time. I know that Jesus lives within and without and that is enough for me. That truth is enough for all men who care to listen and to have faith grow in their hearts as they respond to God's love.

God's love. How can I forget it as I have experienced it so fully that I have thought to burst, so fully that I have felt on fire and capable of healing all brokenness around me? But I do not reach out as I should and the opportunities given to spread this healing power are lost. Lost as so many of those around me truly are.

I know the direction in which I travel even when my pain blinds me, when my brokenness cries out for healing. I sense God's love leading me. Healing always comes, as others listen and reach out, even when I have not. I understand that God loves me even with my brokenness and unwillingness to touch, that my Lord may heal through me.

The direction I travel today leads over that lonely hill. I dread to reach that tree. I have felt as alone as the tree stands. But my Lord commands, and, most of the time, I follow.

There are prairie dog holes and cow droppings littering the landscape, spoiling the "unspoiled beauty of nature." I travel up the hill, and as I get closer to my meeting with the tree, I notice that it has been hit by lightning recently. There is a blackness to it, a charred limb. But it still struggles to life, to crown the lonely hill.

Broken, and yet alive. That describes those who follow Jesus. It is a life that comes from within, which not even the strongest lightning strike can destroy as long as the Spirit is within.

As I gaze at the tree struggling to live, I feel the spirit struggling within me. Struggling to grow, to reach the sky. To reach the source of eternal life which is my Lord Jesus Christ. It is a struggle of light versus darkness, and the darkness in my soul begins to lift and I begin to join with the life around me celebrating rebirth.

A dead, split log nourishes a growing seedling. Soon, there will be two trees upon this hill, no, three, yes, four. Signs of new growth abound upon my "lonely hill."

Coming finally to the top of the hill and to my lonely tree, I sense life that I did not see from the distance. A nest of newly hatched pheasants adorns my "lonely hill", an eagle flies overhead, some deer graze in the plain below; even the ground hogs frolic as they take a break from digging their holes. The tree itself offers sanctuary to another nesting pair. This tree is not alone, nor is it separated from the world around it. And that "smallest leaf" is as connected to the source of life as any other.

Nor am I alone or separated. I belong to the world that I decry as selfish and uncaring. But as I, too, am broken, I may not throw the first rock; rather, I should celebrate the faith which always brings me back to the river of love which flows through those who follow my Lord. That river that brings with it life which is not of this world, and, most essentially, such joy which to feel it causes one to dance.

River of love - one which does not dry up in drought, one that does not permit puny dams or other obstacles made by man to withhold its power from the world it seeks to nourish. I know this as truth. Though evil may surround me, yet this love flows throughout, vanquishing the darkness of the soul from my being. As a river of love, life being called back to the sea, and rainstorms bestowing it upon land again. As a cycle of healing power - from God to us, to Him and yet to us again.

This water of life dances through waterfalls, along streams, joyously celebrating the life it gives - and those who wish to drink of it transform their living, loving life around them.

Power, yes, water crashing onto rocks, the power carving sculptures thereon. As an oyster creates a pearl through pain, yet the water creates beauty, and we who drink help God create ourselves. Yes, the "lonely tree" struggles through life, the decaying log broken, dispirited, yet life comes forth from both, because of both - the tree and its companions truly "crowning" the hill as emissaries of the Lord of Life, of Love.

I, too, wish to spread seeds of the life He has shared with me to the world around me. To act as a beacon, showing true life if one dares to come close enough to see the reflection of His light through me. I wish to dance to the music of the waterfalls, to the quiet streams, the majestic rivers, to all which comes from the source of life that has freed me from the bondage of fear and pain.

As I dance through the world, I have found that others join me when I share the dancing music with them- for the only way to keep this joy is to share it. Such joy cannot be piled up for posterity, or even grasped or held. Nor can one command when it should come and wash away the burdens of this world. But come it does to those who have faith.

When life becomes too much, my despair too heavy to carry, I call to my Lord and he answers. When I drag my feet, my Lord puts music in my heart, and the dance begins once more.

January 2005

Dancing is an important image to me. I think it involves listening to the music and moving in accord with it. For me, the music cmnes from the movement of God's love within my soul, a sure steady stream even when I look away from it. The sound permeates my movement and my being. When I experience joy, I become that sound.

Canine Companions - my story - 2004

I owe much to all my faithful canine companions. I met Tippy, part Golden Retriever and part Saint Bernard, my last year teaching on the Rosebud Indian Reservation. I had broken my leg at the teacher's picnic playing softball. The puppy quickly discovered that lying down solved many problems. This made much sense, as anyone on crutches with a broken leg being greeted by a tied up puppy soon realizes as the excited youngster winds the rope to which it has been tied around you and your crutches. Five years later, it was still Tippy's solution to an immediate crisis. The strange thing is, it often worked, and I would often break out laughing as she confidently plopped herself down with a thud. The louder the thud, the surer she was that lying down would work.

Tippy's presence helped much that first year after my mother died. One of my most vivid memories during that year was the wonderful gift my far-ranging puppy brought back to me. She discovered a dead skunk, and thought, as would many carnivorous beings, it would make a great gift. When she left it on the porch, I said "Thanks," and quickly found an alternative place for it. The next day, the same gift was back again on the porch. Fortunately it was winter, and a South Dakota winter means a deep freeze. I found another place for it, and, again the next day it was on the porch. This time the tail fell off as I moved it. The Golden Retriever that had been Tippy's ancestor would have been proud of her. Fortunately, eventually, Tippy found other things to occupy her.

Later, in the spring, she chased a flock of wild turkeys; she thought that they would make an even better gift than the skunk. Fortunately, she only succeeded in brightening my mood. I was fascinated at how gracefully the turkeys flew down from the trees every morning. But going up the tree to safety at night, they were extremely ungainly, hopping from limb to limb as they went higher up, landing on each branch with an obvious thud.

Tippy had a great sense of motherhood, so much so that when I visited a friend on "Four Wheel Drive Road," she let the resident three-year-old boy stand on top of her without complaint. Fortunately, his mother ran over and grabbed him before he did too much damage to my dog - although I don't think that it was damage to my dog that was worrying her. Anyway, that vacation Tippy saved me from a bee by snapping it out of the air before it could land on me. I was pleased to discover that SHE wasn't allergic to bees as I am. She spent all night awake guarding my pickup from the raccoons - which ate such things as brake linings, and all day awake guarding the kids and the rest of us at the swimming hole. She spent the first three days back home sleeping. My favorite photograph consists of me lying on the couch with Tippy lying on top of me - and my Dad's cat lying on top of Tippy. My Dad's cat had been brought home a bit young - and had decided that Tippy was her mother. Tippy liked having a cat as an adopted daughter.

I adopted Dewey, part Husky and part Border Collie, the first year I was a pastor in northwest Iowa, shortly after the first transient needing help showed up on the parsonage steps. Having attended college in New York City, I was wary of strangers. Dewey helped me to relax and to be open to helping those who showed up in need.

At first, Dewey felt he was a reject because his previous owners had abandoned him at the SPCA, but my congregation soon changed his mind. I took him to the installation of officers of the Women's Fellowship and tied him to a post in the fellowship room in the church basement. During the service, he chewed his way through his lead and came over to me as I led the service. I stood on his lead, and he chewed his way through it again. One of the women beckoned him over and started petting him. When I played my one-handed special on the piano for our hymns, Dewey joined in and howled for the first and only time.

The ladies fussed over him after the service, completing his initiation into his new pack, not for a moment did he lack someone willing to pet him. Needless to say, this episode joined the collection of stories that the church tells about its pastors.

I did not bring the same dog home. Dewey recognized his important job as bodyguard to a very important leader of the pack. Most dog packs have less than ten members; Dewey's had over forty. He was quite impressed with me, and his dedication showed it. He told me when the buzzer on my chicken dinner went off (it would have burned); when my father moved my car without my knowledge; and when the basement didn't quite smell right.

Dewey probably saved my life with this last complaint. I asked the church property committee to check out the heating as I thought that might be what Dewey was complaining about. The furnace hadn't been cleaned in quite some time. The serviceman told me that the furnace had been working at 40% efficiency. Later, I discovered dogs can smell carbon monoxide. I am not sure who "rescued" whom.

Dewey impressed my importance as a pack leader upon the Spirit, my black Lab mix that I adopted after I moved to New York. I now have two devoted bodyguards.

Both dogs considered being petted by members of my churches as part of their job description, as their second most important duty.

Both Dewey and Spirit had experienced abuse in the first "pack" to which they had belonged. They experienced a big change in their lives as they became members of my pack, as I shared the love I have been given with them, as the members of my congregations lavished them with love as well. The mutual experience of love changes all who are open to it.

The Bridge to Everywhere - fiction - 1989

Arf the elf looked around him. He had no idea where he was, didn't recognize a thing, and moreover, didn't care where he was as long as everyone left him alone. Arf noticed that a shroud of fog in the center of an island, twenty feet in diameter, surrounded by what looked like a quicksand barrier, enclosed him. How he had gotten there, he didn't care, nor did he care to think about leaving.

He liked the isolation; it felt safe after the last few years in the hands of his manipulating wife. No bottles to duck, no knives to come swinging through the air when least expected, safety. She had sued him, him the innocent one, and all had believed her story. He'd lost custody of the kids, mutual friends; no one would speak to him after his wife, ex-wife, told her stories. He wasn't convincing when he tried to deny their truthfulness, because her stories were the ones he had wanted to tell and couldn't, of what she had done to him. She'd lied herself blue, and they all had believed. Her, not him. Not a one had believed. He didn't care if he ever found his way back.

He didn't want friends, because friendship hurt; he didn't want love, because it turned into ice, then fire, threatening to consume all it touched. He didn't even want God in his life. That's what he had been thinking as he sat drinking alone the night the divorce became final - and he'd woken up here. Wherever "here" was.

A day, a week, a month and still he liked the isolation. The island started growing smaller, and Arf didn't notice - he still had no trouble finding food to eat. Soon the island was only seven feet across. And Arf began to notice. Notice the quiet. The only other living creature was a tree, which fed him several kinds of fruits and nuts.

A tree whose branches he sat on trying to see farther into the fog - nothing.

But, nothing underfoot either. Just a tree now itself surrounded in fog. He reached out and found the food although he couldn't see it. Something was missing; Arf was beginning to shrivel, to resemble the petrified wood he had dug up while looking for a leprechauns treasure. A hard, dead piece of what might as well be stone rather than something which once was alive. He began to pray the prayer which his mother had taught him as a child, that prayer that always left a feeling of safety and comfort. But still the fog surrounded him.

Time seemed endless, with no way, no reason to measure it. The fog and moat now seemed a merciless trap built just to enclose him. "Mercy, have mercy," he cried. To no one, he thought. God, who had let his wife take everything, no longer had any ears.

A voice came, "Papa, come." Come? To where, from where? How could he leave the one safe spot . . . but the fruit now tasted bitter, the nuts now hard or rotten. "Papa, come," the voice pleaded. Arf knew he'd die if he stayed, but to venture into nothingness because another's voice called? Arf said that prayer again, and a small seed of hope began to grow in his heart.

"Papa, come." Again. How to trust a bodiless voice, when all those he'd trusted before had proved faithless. Arf realized he hadn't much choice as the last nut picked disintegrated as he stared at it. "Papa, come. It's safe, trust me."

Unable to handle being where he was, Arf jumped down and ran twenty-five steps towards the voice until he realized that he was walking on what he had once thought to be quicksand. He stopped, and started to sink. "Trust," the word echoed eerily through the fog. Arf pulled himself up and ran some more, until again he remembered the quicksand, and the pain that had propelled him away from those people he had once loved.

To love again? Trust again? But what choice now did he have - to sink into the sands of oblivion? Not Arf, he'd always been the one never to quit - so why was he quitting now? Repeating his childhood prayer, Arf pulled his foot out, and then the other. "Papa, come. The land is solid, run until you can finally see." The voice was stronger now, but an irritating quality to it reminded him of his ex-wife.

Anger filled Arf, anger - an energy fit to melt the largest iceberg. And that's what the energy began to do.

Arf's petrified heart began to bleed, the pain he'd run from filling it as it thawed. The seed in his heart began to grow, sprouting, watered by the melting anger. Finally, like an iceberg breaking off the glacial shore and trusting itself to the sea, Arf moved, slowly, then quickly as the life spread throughout his body.

"Papa, come." Not his wife, but his son, his son who still loved him, believed in him. He ran, and stepped out into the light. He found himself standing beside his nearly grown son, next to a foggy moat. A sign warned, "Beware the Moat of Forgetfulness. Dark and Dreary. None return."

So that was where he had been! No wonder...his son was half-grown, why... Arf grabbed his son.

"I knew you were different Dad. They kept telling me no one ever comes back, but I didn't believe them. I believed your love for me would bring you back if I called. So once every year I came..."

Once a year? Was that how much time had passed between hearing the voice calling him? It had seemed only moments. Years, it had been fifteen years since he had left, and his son had remembered, had loved him, and had called in faith for him.

"Did you ever find the fishing hole which I was going to show you with the monstrous trout?" Arf asked.

His son grinned, "No, I waited for you to show me."

Arf grabbed his son in a huge hug, encountering warmth and life, the seed in his heart now flowering in its fullness. Father and son walked off, arm in arm, betting which one of them would catch that monster fish that'd be even larger after waiting fifteen years for them to catch it together. The bond between them was now reestablished and stronger. Arf walked with a spring in his step that had never been there before his encounter with the fog.

Having just passed through the Christmas season, I experienced again the power of light. The period between Thanksgiving and Christmas is my least favorite time of year, with the sun filling the sky for a shorter period of time each day. I get gloomy. The Christmas Eve service erases all of this and fills the emptied spaces with peace and joy, as well as a strong anticipation of the life the next year will bring into my life. I find a sermon on Christmas Eve to be anti-climatic and distracting from what is occurring. And so, I tell stories and, just before we sing "Silent Night" while each member of the congregation holds their candle ready to be lit from the light from the Christ candle in our advent wreath, I speak for a moment on "Why We Light our Candles"...

One Candle at a Time - 1/2006 - meditation
Isaiah 9:2, John 1:1-5

Why do we light a candle, now?

Light is important symbol in our worship services. On Good Friday at Tenebrae Service, we snuff out candles one by one, leaving only one still burning; we leave the church with only enough light left to see our way out safely. We go out into the dark night. Then at Easter sunrise services, we celebrate the return of light into our lives more strongly than before as we celebrate the gift of the resurrection. Light is the main theme. But this day, we celebrate the presence of but a few candles, lighting candles one by one, much the opposite of Good Friday.

Imagine a world before electric light, when candles were the only source of illumination after the dark night came. Rarely do we experience such darkness now. When we do, we don't like it. But there is still something special

71

about a candle as it flickers before us; there's still something special about candlelight dinners, and candles at weddings, and yes, candles on Christmas Eve. There is something about these Advent candles that shine in the darkness, which defeat the darkness. Something that cries out to our souls.

This light, this Christ light in our Advent wreath, wants to shine in our dark world. We light our candles because it IS a dark world, and not just because the sun has traveled on. It is so easy to care more for getting our Christmas dinners and presents ready on time than to care for those who cannot afford those luxuries. And there are so many people hidden within our lives who can't. And there are also many dark places within our own lives and hearts. This light wants to shine in our dark world.

But is the world really so dark? And why must we dwell on such depressing gloom tonight of all nights, this night when we want to be so happy? Candles, for all their beauty, don't give a huge amount of light. When the power goes off at night in your home, light a candle and you will see what I mean. Light six or eight candles, there is still only a faint glow. Candles do nothing to light a fully illuminated room; can one candle be so important? Can our one candle be important at all?

In the depth of darkness, one candle can still make a difference between life and death. Why do we light our candles? Because we want, need light. Darkness makes us truly appreciate light.

But this night, we start with the Christ candle. When we blow out the flame of our candle as we leave, the light is still present. If we want it to be still present; if we have room for the presence of Christ in our lives.

The light is still present.

Why do we light the candles? Because, despite the darkness, we yearn for light.

Power goes out in our homes during a winter ice storm. We grope, stumbling about. Someone finally finds a match, snap, lights a candle, and there is light. Relief floods the faces of those in the room.

Every year, on Good Friday night, we celebrate Tenebrae. Seven candles upon the altar are extinguished one by one. And when the last candle goes out it is dark, very, very dark. Then one candle is lit. One little candle upon the altar, and the whole place seems to glow. A fragile light, yes, but this light is the light of Christ's love, that love that defeats all darkness.

Isn't that why we light our candles?

The light of the candle each of us will light tonight will still be present when we go out; if we want it to be; if we have room for the presence of Christ in our lives.

The light is still present.

Why do we light our candles? Because the light shines in the darkness and the darkness, two thousand years later, thank God, has not overcome it.

We have not come just to light candles tonight, but to celebrate the presence of the light of Christ in our world. We come here tonight because there is something within us, something that rises, warms to the glow of Christmas candles, strengthens with the singing of our carols, and gathers inspiration with the reading of our lessons. We do come, on this night of all nights, because we want to celebrate. And celebrate we should. Celebrate the presence of the light of the world within us and about us.

And so the lighting begins, as I light this one candle of mine with the light of the Christ candle. And the lighting continues as I share my light with you, and you share your light with the person next to you. And the lighting continues until the candles of all who are within this church are lit. And the darkness diminishes and leaves. This one candle of mine could not do it. But a church full of lit candles is quite different. Very different as the light of the candles light up each face, lights up each heart within. And so, when we go out, we can share the light of Christ's love with the world around us. Then this time, next year, the world will not be so dark.

Isn't that why we light our candles?

The light of the candle each of us will light tonight will still be present when we go out; if we want it to be; if we have room for the presence of Christ in our lives.

The light is still present.

Why do we light our candles? Because the light shines in the darkness and the darkness has not overcome it.

On Christmas Eve - my story - January 2006

I can't decide which has more power for me, Christmas or Easter. Christmas celebrates the divine presence of Christ traveling with us. Easter celebrates that joy that we experience through transformation and the promise of even greater joy at some point in the future. The power of both times helps fuel my faith.

Traveling through the Christian church year from Christmas to Easter each year is a powerful cycle; we travel through darkness with the presence of divine light to guide us; we reach greater light and greater joy. Then again we make the journey, each time arriving at a place filled with greater light and joy.

This is why Psalm 126 is my favorite Psalm as it speaks of that cycle. People who "sow in tears" truly do reap with "cries of joy."

This cycle has been my life story. At some points in the cycle, the candles of Christmas that proclaim the presence of Christ's light in the world have had the greater power. At others, the joy that comes with a taste of the resurrection fills my eyes so that I have no need for candles to help me see. This book speaks of that cycle.

Dancing into Joy: Transforming Our Darkness into Light

Movement Four - The Darkness

January 2005

There are many forms of darkness: distrust, pain that burdens the spirit, self-pity, self-hatred, guilt that makes us feel unworthy to be loved, anger with the urge to destroy, and, of course, fear. All these things form "light-blocks" in our spirit that limit the amount of divine light that can enter. They form dams in the river of life and limit who we are and who we can become. They close our hearts and limit the amount of joy that can enter. All these light-blocks limited my experience of God's love when I began my journey of healing. I spent much time dealing with these.

As each memory returned, I would find a new piece of myself, moving nine steps ahead. Then I would have to deal with the emotions that came with it, and I would find myself moving five steps back. The self-hatred, the anger, the self-pity, the fear - all that I felt at the time that that incident had occurred would come back to be processed for the first time. Some of it would roll out of me and away, and some would linger. I would move from liking myself to hating myself; work hard and come to like myself again. Then another piece would come back that was filled with self-hatred and I would start all over again. After awhile, I did not fall down the well of self-hatred when the memories returned. Moving up and down was hard work, but each time I moved upwards more of me was there to love when I reached the top. Each time up, the world was more color-filled and alive. Each time up, greater joy filled my life. It was as if the pieces of newly found joy fueled my determination to integrate as many parts of myself as I could, so I could experience love as fully as I could.

Throughout it all, I wondered about evil and the people who had hurt me so, those creatures of darkness that feared the light. This movement holds much of the wondering and trying to make sense of that which does not make sense - why people choose darkness when the light is so warm and bright.

Hell - my story - April 2005

I have one distinct memory from before I found God under the bed and experienced God's love. I was sitting on the steps after having been told how much I wanted to go to heaven by all sorts of people. I didn't want to go to heaven. I was afraid. I was sure that if I went to heaven God would be watching me, and would catch me doing something wrong – and send me to hell. I felt it would be better starting out in hell in the first place.

At that point in time, I expected punishment as my due – horrible punishment as my due. Before I found God under the bed, my life was filled with fear and darkness.

A Slave to Anger – fiction - April 2005

How could this man be the Messiah? I have followed John these many years, yearning for the Coming One. Yearning for the one sent by God to put these Roman dogs in their place. To give back to them some of the pain and suffering that they have inflicted upon the chosen people of God, the pain they have inflicted upon me.

Those accursed Romans travel through our land, knocking aside our poor and our widows. They take what they want and call it requisitioning, saying their quartermaster will pay. But they do not pay, until after the child of the widow dies, dies because they took her last bit of flour. They feel that the fewer of us there are, the better. What does a denarii mean to a widow whose child is dead? Can the dead child eat it and come back to life?

I have followed John with his baptism of repentance, whose booming voice scared those who had lost their way into coming back to the holy faith. John who preached that those who commit sin would get their just due. And now he tells me to follow this Jesus.

Does this Jesus care what the Romans do? He tells us to give to Caesar what belongs to Caesar – Israel does NOT belong to Caesar, but to the Lord. The Lord compels us to rise up against these Romans who defile our faith, these Romans who want us to worship their Emperor as if he were the Lord, our God. They want us to worship that one who only cares for himself, who encourages his people to take more from us. The one we are truly called upon to worship cares. The Lord cries for each widow who is left alone when the Romans kill her zealot husband. The Lord cries when our leaders do as the Romans ask rather than obey the scriptures of our Fathers.

This Jesus wants to heal my anger and pain; he wants to heal that pain that comes from the suicide of my wife. My dear wife whose only fault was to be beautiful around drunken Romans. I want my anger. It gives me a reason to live. It gives me reason to seek the Messiah who will save our land from those who defile it. The Messiah will come, for the Lord has promised.

This Jesus has caused a child to rise from the dead they say; he has caused his friend Lazarus to come forth from the tomb alive. Even should I have seen these things with my own eyes, I would not believe. I would refuse to believe, for they say he has healed the servant of a centurion as well. A Roman occupier! This Jesus is a fake if he will not demand vengeance for the dead of the Lord. This Jesus is a blasphemer worse than the Romans who wish to enter our temple to satisfy their curiosity about our "strange" faith.

They have arrested him, I hear. The servants of the priests are coming among those of us who are poor and hungry. Not to give us the food and help as commanded by the Lord. No, they want something from us, something that I, for one, will be pleased to give for free. They are asking us to come to Pilate's presentation, to yell for the crucifixion of this Jesus. They offer us "poor" pickings from what has been offered to the priests as payment.

I do not need to be bribed to yell to crucify this fake Messiah, for this Jesus who proclaims love to the Romans and Samaritans is a blasphemer who deserves to die. It will be a privilege to do as the priests ask. It will be a privilege to help rid Jerusalem of one who can only cause it greater harm. My anger will proclaim the falseness of this one who preaches love rather than vengeance. My anger will be fulfilled.

Darkness - meditation - 1989

The darkness, what can be said of it?

We have all seen some of those people who, possessed by the soul of darkness, stumble through a pain-filled universe, driven by a desire, no, a need, to punish themselves for their feebleness, their powerlessness as life rushes by them. They have accepted the promises of darkness, that blindness is peace, that destroying eases pain, that oblivion eases loneliness. That promise is true, temporarily. If one does not see one's brokenness and hides in the darkness instead, one does not have the struggle of accepting the pain. Finding, controlling another victim eases the rapist's pain of powerlessness for a moment with the drug of imagined powerfulness. But, the rapist's soul receives the added guilt of yet another victim, yet another reason to condemn the self, yet another load of pain, another foot added to the gulf of loneliness between the rapist and the world of life.

And oblivion? What is that but the act of being alone, without God or man, in the darkness of a dying soul?

The heavier the load of guilt we give ourselves, the harder it is to forgive ourselves. Responding to pain destructively adds yet more pain, loneliness and fear, not only in the heart of the perpetrator, but also in that of the victim.

How many victims hold onto imagined guilt, feeling that they deserve what has happened, as a reason not to reach out and trust, not to take the risk of loving others? They, too, hating themselves fall into the morass of darkness.

Darkness. A black hole created by life falling in on itself, withdrawing so that nothing, not even God's healing love, can pierce that "protective" armor.

Darkness, self-destruction, is chosen by many people in this world in varying degrees, a fact which I find that I cannot comprehend. I can only mourn, mourn the lost opportunities of receiving life, of accepting God's love, of experiencing joy.

Many of us temporarily reside in darkness when we lose someone we love. We find ourselves in darkness when our world comes crashing down as the prelude to transformative healing. It isn't the same darkness. This is the darkness of the caterpillar's cocoon rather than the darkness of the cave.

Those who choose the cave of darkness, choose it without the presence of God traveling with them. They choose it to hide from God, as if anything they do can deny them the reality of God's love. All that they truly do is hide the presence of God from their own eyes.

Darkness Inconceivable - my story - May 2006

As I was arranging this book, I noticed that I didn't have enough "My Story" pieces in this section - so I tried to write one. I can't put myself in the mental space to write something that fits in here. My world is no longer dark enough to speak of living in darkness in a present day voice.

Back in the mid 1980's, my world was dark with spots of light: light in my heart, light in the faces of the people who reached out to me. Now, my world is bright with spots of darkness. Dancing has been good to me.

The darkness that I wrote about then - and in which I lived - is hard for even me to imagine. It wasn't until last week that I found a "darkness" in my present day about which to write.

I don't mean that darkness doesn't bother me. I just don't live in it anymore. With all the healing I have experienced, I've gotten the idea that healing and growth just keep happening; that if you open yourself up to the power of God's love, you just keep growing and becoming more. I've gotten the sense that there is never a time of diminishment, only of growth.

But this past week, I performed a funeral for someone five years younger. I've done that once before, for a college student who committed suicide. I could shrug off a college student's suicide, and funerals for older people didn't bother me. This one was different.

The person from my Belfield congregation who died was full of life; she had experienced transformation dealing with cancer. She was fully alive - but she died. She didn't do anything silly, such as drink and drive. She was a responsible adult, loved by many. At her funeral, I preached to the largest congregation in my career, with around 600 present. These hundreds of people gave testimony to how fully alive she had spent her life.

I experienced a bit of culture shock when I went to the funeral home to lead an informal prayer service for the family. I discovered that people in North Dakota have a different definition of family than I had found in New York State. More than 250 people were sitting waiting for me. In New York, that many rarely show up for the funeral. I led an impromptu funeral, rather than the New York style prayer service I had planned.

The next day, I headed out to the funeral that was taking place in an unused school about 30 miles away. As I got on Interstate 94 an hour and a quarter before the funeral, I found myself in a traffic jam. Construction had slowed people down, and at least one person in front of me was NOT in a hurry to get where they were going. For the first time in a long time, I was surrounded by at least twelve cars. My culture shock from the evening before began to wear off.

Once out of construction, I passed those who were going 10 miles below the speed limit. I was concerned about finding the school, as the only directions I had were, "go to the next exit after Belfield." At the "next exit after Belfield" all except one of the cars exited. I followed the cars to the school. When I entered the gym just before the funeral, my culture shock returned as I faced six hundred people. I opened my heart and spoke of 1 Corinthians 13 as I often do at funerals. This passage about love is the best gift I can offer at either funerals or weddings.

But this fully alive person died. I now realize that there will come a time when I no longer grow into more than I have been. Time is keeping count, even if I am not. This is a different type of darkness.

I am reminded, again, of Psalm 126, which states that those who sow in tears will reap with cries of joy. The Psalm ends with a strong harvest imagery. The person whom we become with the help of God's love is the person who experiences the harvest. We experience a harvest here and now as we dance with the taste of joy. But we also experience a harvest as did this woman who died last week. We experience the harvest of the love of our friends and family at our death; we experience the harvest of God's love that we have allowed ourselves to experience while here on earth. And we experience the harvest of the fullness of joy that comes with the actual resurrection.

The darkness I found myself in last week is defeated by death. And death has already been defeated by the resurrection.

To Trust... Again - (1989)

Darkness breaks delicate things
the bonds of friendship
the stirrings of life
the ability to trust the truth.

Darkness enfolds, attempting to bind
to imprison the will to live, to love.
What matter in life to one
who cannot speak of truth hidden away
who cannot smell roses in spring -
but can only smell the sludge in winter,
who cannot hear laughter in ocean waves -
only pain as they break on the beach,
who cannot see love, cannot reach out,
cannot touch the things of life.

But darkness is itself afraid,
of life, of love, of truth.
Darkness is itself a prisoner
enclosed in a void of loneliness.

Risking, reaching out
searching for truth
vanquishing that cloak of darkness
enclosing my heart no more.
Hope plants seeds of love,
tears water
and joy brings forth new life.

Hesitating, hope-filled, risking all
once to trust
once to touch, to hear, to see,
to know at last the truth.

For once becomes a habit
And we travel a different path
together.

Promises Broken and Promises Kept - 1989

My heart aches, for a promise broken
a promise implied, never stated,
but a promise still.

As a mother promises the child she bears safety,
As a dad promises the child he helps create warmth,
clothing and shelter, nourishment,
Promises not stated, but of nature made,
Not kept as self-seeking fears pain, truth.

My heart aches for that which I lost,
never safety to feel, coldness and nakedness
my birthright.

My heart aches, for a promise seems broken
made by my Lord, my God.
If I trust those He chooses life would
transform, joyous exaltation be mine
for once.
Not the pain, loneliness that fills me.
true not as I once felt such,
but still my trust is shaken-
for the first time since told to trust.

Pain, loneliness.

I want the promised land.
I want to dance in the dewdrops of dawn,
I want to act in my Lord's pageant of love.

And so I shall continue to trust as told.
I shall hope against logic as I listen,
hope as I have since I began my search,
search for people, to trust-
to love with the frozen river of love
still inside, which flows from my Lord to me, and
hopefully some day, flowing freely
to the world around me.

But pain, loneliness chills my heart.

Yes, my Lord felt such himself on a cross,
for to love man is to love imperfection,
limited, often broken, hate filled, fearful beings,
But with love-all share in His Life.

And wishing a share of life, of joy,
I follow my Lord's promise,
I shall allow my river to thaw
from the fire of faith gifted to me,
send my river to nourish the hungry
the parched and broken
as my Lord commands me,
Someday to dance in joy,
as I share the bountiful gifts of
my Lord, my God.

Amen.

This piece shows the power of being in love with God, as that power drew me out of myself. My love for God made me reach out, and God's love for me allowed me to take the risk of so doing.

Rejoice in the Lord Always - prose poem - 1989

Lord, I want to rejoice, but I cannot. I wish to sing of your love, which surrounds me, but I am mute. I want to tell of the wonders of your saving power, but fear overwhelms me as I begin to speak. Lord, You have transformed me, but I still tremble in fear as I face the world around me.

I have always tried to follow You, Lord; tried to follow the path as You have led me - waiting patiently when I stopped - helping lovingly when I stumbled, never leaving me even when I would not look at You. Often, You held my hand as we traveled; held me and guided me as I walked with my eyes tightly shut, too afraid to look at where I was going.

Lord, I want to tell of the miracles you have shared with me: of beautiful sounds sung with joy; of friends who helped you to heal; of a people warm and generous.

Lord, I want to tell of the people You have shared with me, of people so full of love for You that a bright, warm flame seems to glow from deep within them. Of one, blind in earthly matters, whose voice praises you in marvelous song, sharing the gift of the vision you have given her. Of others, poor in earthly matters whose arms enfold and heal your people, sharing the rich gift of the Love You have given them.

Lord, I am thirsty, tired, gripped by the pain of my fears. I have traveled through a wilderness in which I did not recognize myself. I have traveled through a fierce fire that burned and took away that which was not truly me. Throughout, Lord, I have recognized you: Your love for me has never wavered; your love lighted my path; often, your love was the only familiar part of my world. I have held onto my faith, transformed, and become truly free.

Yet, I am still in a desert. I try to sing, but my voice falters, from heat or fear, I know not which. I am filled with faltering joy; as if the joy were newly born, newly learning how to walk, and some day to run. One day, Lord, I will sing your praises in a clear, strong voice. One day, Lord, You will send a river to transform this desert I live in, which the world around me may share my joy in you.

A Light in the Darkness – prose poem - 1989

I am afraid of the dark, Lord. It scares me to death, I cannot move - cannot leave this frail candle of your love that I hold. This small light is sure and safe and lights the space around me, but it is so small. I see your fire shining far away, a fire much brighter than my small light. A bonfire warming all it touches. To reach the brightness of your fire, I have to travel through the darkness that surrounds me

But the path is rocky, dark and steep. I fear to travel upwards, I fear I will stumble and fall. No light shows but your fire, my candle, and some few others scattered throughout the darkness. It is so warm here. How can I leave this sanctuary to follow your call further? But is this perceived sanctuary really that, or is it a prison?

I am the candle. Once I had no fire in my heart. My heart was frozen. Then you came and lit my faith. Your sacrifice and grace lit my dark soul. I am no longer a captive of the darkness. You called me to die to this darkness, and then to burst forth with new life into the world of light, becoming like a fireworks display showering the dark night with the beauty of light and of truth.

But - I fear my light will die, as do the fireworks when burnt out by the burst of light. The darkness outside, steel curtains nothing can breathe in, a prison, which lets nothing, move against its will.

But I, I am the candle. Showering the life given to me by your sacrifice throughout my sanctuary, making it a place of light, keeping hate and its coldness out in the darkness, sending my light through, sending it out, to warm all that it touches. This light you have given me cannot be conquered unless I let go of it, unless I drop it. That I will never do. I will tend my flame. I will never become a prisoner of darkness again.

I am that candle, Lord. The flame of faith warms me when I feel faint and cold. As I move through that darkness, towards you, my Lord, my flame grows. I find some of your people, and we share the warmth of our candles, together creating a sanctuary from the darkness. Others come into our sanctuary, searching for the warmth that we willingly share with them - too often they left, not accepting what they have found - searching for something they can see and touch, and they freeze in the darkness, alone. Others accept what you have given us to share, and leave with candles of their own. They join in the journey, and we tend our flames, sharing, moving towards you, and you save our souls.

The Fire that Burns the Soul - fiction - 1989

The man with the bow tie pulled the gold to himself from across the table. It was the biggest pot of the game. Even bigger than the one last week.

Last week he had played with Evan Parker. The man grinned, his bow tie bouncing as he relished the thought-Parker had lost his shirt. The fool had asked for a loan to feed his children. He had enjoyed watching Parker's face as he had said, "No, I choose not to." The man laughed. Parker had even had to steal the rope he had used to hang himself.

The man with the bow tie had sewn those winnings into the lining of his coat since he couldn't fit any more into his mattress and chairs. He reached into his pocket and felt the bulky lining. He'd done it several times since winning the money. He liked the feel of it close to his skin. The man loved controlling money, games, and people.

As he pulled the gold to himself, the others left the table, they had had enough-but the man did not notice as he fondled and shined each gold piece to a high gloss. The harder he worked, the greater the emptiness within grew.

He rose from the table feeling desperate, not knowing what he wanted. He noticed his reflection in the mirror. Not his gaunt, hungry face or his empty eyes did he see, but rather his bow tie - another trophy in his game of dominance. It had belonged to his brother who had owned half of both the town bank and the house he now lived in, his brother discredited and long since dead.

With sudden dislike, he tore off the bow tie and threw it into the fire next to him. He sat down hoping to feel the fire's warmth, but the coldness within him grew instead. He lit several candles, so he could see his money better, ripped open his mattress, his chairs, placing all his hidden wealth on the table, searching, searching - not finding near enough to satisfy.

Then he lit several more candles, sat down to count his hoard he grew sleepy-and lit more candles so he could better see-continuing to count, piling gold piece upon gold piece. The desperation in his heart keeping him awake as the candles burnt low. Soon the man found himself staring at the light reflecting off the gold in front of him.

The glow grew as one of the candles ignited a forgotten hundred-dollar bill. He felt the growing warmth and stared at the growing light reflecting off the gold. This was what he had been searching for, the man thought, staring at the gold, hypnotized.

One by one, then hundreds by hundreds, the paper money ignited and joined the flames. Soon the table, the room, the entire house was ablaze, but the man still stared, feeling a type of ecstasy he had never felt before.

The next morning, neighbors found the charred remains of the house, the man and his money. The gold had melted in the heat and encased the remains of the man. Unable to separate the two and quite unwilling to try, the townspeople buried the man and his gold in a forgotten, already haunted corner of the graveyard, the man forever joined with his gold.

Dancing Fever – my story - April 2005

I distinctly remember one case of spring fever that I had in 1987. I had "woken up" as described in "And I Shall Dance this Way Again" that previous summer, so I was becoming increasingly alive almost daily. I was constantly stretching my boundaries. More feelings were filling my heart each week than I had thought could ever fit within it. Each day, something new happened, something through which I experienced more of myself than I ever had before. Everyday life was a time of discovery.

On this particular day, I was at work, trying to get the computer programs to act as I thought they should be able to act - and - although I knew the answer to success was sitting around the corner I just couldn't concentrate. I didn't care how many extra addresses my employers sent their propaganda to thereby wasting money, I didn't care even that it was payday. I couldn't sit. My backside wanted to dance and would NOT sit. The world seemed far too new to experience it from inside a concrete box called a business park. Whatever did concrete have to do with life?

I tried for the twentieth time. Failed for the twentieth time. I tried for the thirtieth time, and failed - again. So I gave up trying to fit into someone else's story. I told my boss that I just could not stay and left. He actually gave me permission to go - and even gave me my paycheck. I stuck it in my pocket and went on to better things. Out I went into the sunshine.

There were flowers all around whose names I had never been able to learn. Many differently textured yellow flowers. Other colors whose flowered names I had not bothered to discover. If you don't fully live in the world because it hurts too much, there are many things you don't learn, many things that you don't see or hear or taste or smell - and certainly many things you never feel. There are many things that only have meaning if you are really alive.

I was in a new world filled with shapes and colors and textures - and even smells. Light itself seemed brighter. I wandered around in spring for what felt the first time in my life for hours. I lost my paycheck (which my employer fortunately replaced) and found more of myself.

Later, I discovered the cause. For the first time in my life, I trusted the world enough to stop expecting someone to jump out of nowhere and hurt me; I stopped expecting that the bad and the painful would always happen. Darkness no longer ruled the substance of my life. That day was truly a case of dancing fever.

April 2005

The darkness is scary, and it is no wonder that many people get lost in it. I would hate to think back and list the times I almost got lost in it. But God stands before us the whole time we are lost, telling us not to fear; telling us if we could but open our eyes and trust, the light would be there to guide us out.

Movement Five - Choosing Life, Rejecting Darkness

November 2004

We make decisions about how our life will turn out long before the effects of those decisions are seen. In moments of crisis, we tend not to have the time to sit, reflect and make a reasoned choice. We respond as we have taught ourselves to respond through decisions we have made beforehand. If we have decided through our previous actions that we will not forgive or that we are too weak to face our fears, when the crisis comes we do not have the spiritual muscles to make a different choice. It is often in our times of quiet that we make our decision as to how we will react in a crisis. Our decisions and our strength of will are very important during our times of quiet. During the crisis we act as we have programmed ourselves to act.

If, in our times of quiet, we program ourselves to seek the light, then when anger fills us we know what to do with it. If, in our times of quiet, we seek the presence of the light in our lives, then when the darkness of fear overwhelms us that light is present within us to show us the path.

If we choose the life most filled with light, that life will be ours.

Dancing Practice - my story - 2005

I made a significant life changing decision in seventh grade. I looked at the kids around me in school and did not understand them at all. Their games made no sense. Their erratic friendships made no sense.

I was afraid to call them on the phone. I looked at them making decisions like kids, making and choosing friends like kids, and did not understand at all - I was no kid at that time. But I decided to get to know them. I did not wish to live isolated and alone. And so I chose to begin my journey through healing when I had no idea of that which I was deciding.

I made this decision in the quiet of my lonely room. The only dancing partners that I had had at this point were my dog Ginger and the Christ who had "fixed" me as a child. They danced well, but somehow they were not enough. I wanted to dance with some of those other strange creatures in my world.

I have to admit that I enjoyed my dog. We were strongly bonded, as I had nursed her through the distemper that she had had when we brought her home from the pet store when I was in fourth or fifth grade. She would often talk with me, and we had lively conversations, but I still wanted to understand my contemporaries. Conversing with a dog, no matter how intelligent, wasn't quite enough. I needed to seek out people. And so I did.

I am still an introvert, but no longer PAINFULLY so. I found people with whom to dance the dance of being alive, some who danced well and others who didn't. In college, I became part of the newly developing Campus

Team Ministry and part of its music ministry. I even learned to play the spoons.

Each time I reached out became easier. Each time I began to dance, I got better. Each time I did this, the fear that resided inside me diminished. I did not get from being afraid of the telephone to the pulpit in one step, but from many, often quite small, steps. My two congregations now think of me as a dynamic preacher who refuses to let them sleep too much on Sunday mornings. I don't mind a SHORT nap, though.

When I get up and preach and am so filled with energy that I cannot stand still behind the lectern, it is difficult to imagine that I was once afraid to call another 7th grader on the telephone. But I have made many choices in between that brought me out of the darkness of fear and into the light.

Yes, or No - fiction - 1989

"Yes, or no, yes or no, boring questions from boring people. I wish they'd go away and leave me alone," and so Lois slammed the door on her visitors and returned to her kitchen to finish her drink in peaceful solitude.

Today, she'd started a bit early, the first time she'd started drinking before noontime, but her friends weren't coming over that afternoon, so she felt no reason to wait. It just meant, Lois mused, that she wouldn't have to listen to Jean counting the number of times she refilled her glass - boring busybody!

Lois had been drinking daily since the death of her son Philip, killed in a car wreck after storming out of the house after they had argued over his drinking. Her fault really, should have left the boy alone. The alcohol was helpful, cutting the pain that filled her every time she passed his room.

She filled her glass again, to deflect her thoughts, and savored the smooth warmth floating down her throat. Numbness replaced the pain as she filled and emptied the glass again, and again.

"Yes or no? " Suzy repeated to the people at her door. "Why, yes, certainly I'll come." With that she gently closed the door and returned to her morning meditations. Suzy worked hard to change her life, day-by-day, and sometimes even moment-by-moment when the past was too closely with her. It was hard to notice the improvements herself, but her group helped and encouraged. Why, last year she wouldn't have even talked to the people at her door, let alone accept their invitation.

As she sat in the overstuffed chair, her eyes flickered over the poster on the wall. "God grant me the serenity to accept," she repeated, a feeling of warm security flowing through her as she began to seek God's guidance in her life.

Seeking You, My Lord - 1989

Lord, once I traveled up a high mountain,
Others laughed when I told them of my quest
For I was seeking You, in Your Glory,
Seeking You.
I met a chasm I could not cross,
Fear shook the courage from my heart
I turned, determined to try again,
Seeking You.

Lord, once I traveled across a weary desert,
Others laughed when told of whom I sought
For I was seeking You, Your Faithfulness,
Seeking You.
I met a day I could not endure,
Thirst shook determination from my heart,
I turned, hoping to try again-
Loving You.

Lord, once I traveled a cold, painful road,
Others laughed and called me "fool",
For I was seeking You, Your Warmth, Your Love,
Seeking you.
I met a day my smile froze,
Hatred shook hope from my heart,
I turned, I fled-
Seeking You.

Lord, once I traveled, I thought, alone,
For others laughed and walked away
They would not see You there with me-
Holding, helping, leading me.
For I was wrong, I was not alone,
Your love was always with me
My fears you calmed, my thirst you slaked
My hatred You turned to Love.

I meet Your promise wherever I seek-
Promise of love and grace.
I meet Your promise wherever I turn-
Finding always You.

What Choice is There? - 1989

Frozen water
a promise of life
perhaps, someday.

A frozen stream
a promise of life
 of hope this day.

Perhaps.

To stay frozen
confront nature-My heart concurs
but refuses to melt,
to let hope thaw, inspire.

A stubborn heart, bruised unto death,
yet will not accept that either.

Choice is oft fearful,
yet the lack thereof
does indeed choose death.

What choice, someday, is mine?

November 2004

I have always been fascinated by stories and poetry that speak about choice and human freedom. In high school, I was fascinated with Robert Frost's poem speaking of the two roads - and the suggestion that the speaker's life was determined by the choice made. Later, in college, the absolute sense of freedom experienced by the underground man in the writings of Dostoyevsky was what fascinated me. My senior project was Russian literature, for which I read over 10,000 pages of primary material. I affirmed my right and ability to make decisions of my own from a very young age. As I have grown older, I have come to understand that we are not quite as free as I would have wished. But our ultimate expression of freedom is the "yes" or "no" that we say to God's love as it is showered upon us. It is by using the power of that love within our lives that we become more than we were. As it says someplace - "with God all things are possible."

The Road to Peace - 1989

Frozen, afraid, angry, and vengeful.
Why me-
Why me-
Frozen, pained, angry, and vengeful.

Two roads-   to become a storm of ice,
   freeze what I touch, teach how to hate-
   stop the flowing stream before it feeds the valley
    break leafed limbs off trees
    weighted with too much sorrow.

Two roads-   to will to be different
   embrace what I hate, learn how to love-
   stop the spread of death before it consumes the
world
    water the encroaching desert
    with the life of forgiveness.

Two roads-   which one to take
  to determine the way a life will grow-
  a deserted stump of a broken tree
   not even fit to build a fire-
   a tall giant of wood, embracing the forest
    sheltering, encouraging of life,
    giving inspiring warmth even in death.

Two roads-   a personal decision
  to determine the way a world will glow
   a radioactive lump of clay, diseased - dead
  a life-filled light spreading throughout the universe.

A decision, mine.

Fear's Stories - my story - January 2005

The stories told to me by fear, stories telling of how people would hurt me if I trusted them, have proven mostly false. Not completely. There is a strange phenomenon that, once you have been victimized well and thoroughly, you tend to be victimized again. It is as if you wear a neon sign on your forehead that states "I am a victim." Strangers who need someone to victimize in order to feel more powerful in their own lives look for people wearing these signs. "Victims" with signs usually don't tell - they have been trained not to do so. Such people are "safe" to pick on and victimize once again. The victims can't tell as they have been well trained not to, often threatened with violence to those they love should the truth ever come out of their mouths. The perpetrators get away with their violence once again.

This experience trains those who have been victimized to never trust, not even God; for if God loved them why ever would they be so treated? Unless, of course, they deserve it. But then, how to believe that God loves them?

This is not an easy problem to solve. But somehow the radical freedom of the universe enters into it. Others are as free to hurt me, as I am NOT to hurt them in return. Logic cannot satisfy, only the experience of being bathed in God's love can – and even then a certain dissatisfaction lingers. And fear tries to multiply that dissatisfaction into distrust again.

I learned to trust by listening to the five-year-old part of me that was sitting in God's lap. "Trust this person," I would whisper to myself – and that person would prove trustworthy. I would trust the piece of God that I sensed in that person, not the person himself or herself. The five-year old part of me has done a good job helping me grow into adult faith. Eventually, I learned whom not to trust, and the neon sign on my forehead slowly stopped blinking, and eventually was removed.

Fear's stories of how even God would prove false have been proven increasingly false, as my faith and trust in God has increased. I can state this day that I no longer wear that sign - and that I trust people for themselves.

November 2004

I have also been fascinated by how the same thing can work in two different ways at the same time. This poem was inspired by the fire in Yellowstone National Park, the result of which I saw in the summer of 1989 when I traveled out to Idaho during my summer vacation. The meditation that follows it also speaks of choice. I think this was a dominant theme for me at the time that I wrote it because I was choosing to really reach out. Not only was I in seminary, but also I was speaking my mind in my classes and learning much about my fellow students in conversations in the cafeteria.

Friend or Foe? - 1989

I.

Fire, friend or foe?
My Heart calls it foe
as the prairies blacken.
    The pheasants mourn
as the world they know dies.
Fire-it burns with heat
        melting, consuming.
    It blinds with light
        maiming, destroying.

My soul calls it friend
as cold winter loses.
        people revive
as the world they know unfreezes.
Fire-it nourishes with heat
        healing, sustaining.
    It reveals with light
        embracing, creating.

II.

Pain, friend or foe?
My heart calls it foe
as it fills me to bursting.
    My hopes disintegrate
as the world I know dies.

Pain-it scars with heat
        cutting, overwhelming.
    It shows with light
        betraying, killing.

My soul calls it friend
as it is cleansed of weeds.
    My vision clears
as the world I know deepens.
Pain-it molds with heat
    firing, strengthening.
    It blesses with light
    revealing, creating.

III.

Nature plays two parts together-
what destroys also creates
    a loss has a gain.
A charring regenerates-
some seeds need firing to grow-
a balance, a rhythm, a paradox.

Day needs night,
heat needs cold,
life needs death,
and joy needs pain to fully come to birth.

IV.

Life must be kindled
and tended with care.
The birth pangs of the soul,
not welcomed perhaps-
but accepted at least-
usher in capacity for Joy.
And life needs Joy.
to be worth the living.

Vision II - meditation - 1989

Lord, do I really want to let you into my life? To let you come fully into me, to let your love permeate my actions?

I hear others singing of the peace and joy which you bring to them. I see them run dancing through the streets sharing your love with the city. And I watch as ashes transform into sunshine; broken people becoming prophets of joy; abused, neglected children finding safety and love in the arms of strong people; flowers breaking through filth and smog to greet the sun. And I see the rain washing all things clean, giving life, transforming the world around me.

But that rain comes from tears.

Joy does not live without sorrow. Lovers often see the beloved die. Prophets often dance and sing on burning coals. Men often destroy what they do not understand, and only you, Lord, truly understand love. Even you, Jesus, you yourself were broken before the world rejoiced with you on Easter morning.

Is this joy you offer truly worth feeling the pain that comes before it?

And so you answer me with the touch of your hand. A most painful spot in my heart, long hidden, becomes quiet. A scream ringing in my ears that I would not acknowledge becomes still. And I listen and I see.

I see a crippled child painfully accepting his lot and pulling himself out of bed for the first time. I see his determination to succeed, to live a full life. I hear a deer call mournfully for her lost fawn, and sounds of joy as they are reunited.

I see a woman painfully giving birth. I see that pain forgotten as she holds her first born close to her heart. I hear a siren bringing one of yours, Lord, to a hospital where

114

doctors work to no avail - and I hear a cry of joy as you call him by name and he runs into your outstretched arms.

Life does not come without pain, and joy does not come without life.

Lord, I do not want to walk through life as if dead, I want to be alive, to feel. If that means I shall feel pain, then so be it. But it also means I shall be filled with your Joy.

Lord, teach me to dance.

I wrote this story just before I became a volunteer teacher on the Pine Ridge reservation in South Dakota, another reaching out my part to others that healed me as much as the other person was healed. I have found that it often happens this way. When you reach out to touch someone in need and some deep hurting place inside you is healed as well.

The man in the Black Suit - fiction - 1989

The man in the black suit dealt again. As the cards slid across the table, his fellow players methodically picked them up and surveyed them. Nothing flickered across their faces as they looked at their cards, no emotions showed in their voices as they began the betting. The dealer seemed out of place and alone, until he, too, picked up the cards and began to bet. A true player, the man in the black suit allowed nothing to show how he felt about the hand he had been dealt.

As the men placed money and then more money in the center of the table, an empty-eyed child wandered through the maze of tables and stopped, watching the men intently, staring into the faces of the players, one by one. Lastly he looked into the face of the man in the black suit, he stared into this face for quite some time.

The man couldn't help notice, and their eyes met for a few moments, distracting him, breaking his train of thought. The others automatically dealt him out as he confronted the boy's stare. But the man turned back to the game, and the boy continued his search, wandering throughout the room, searching, asking a man now and then if he had seen his daddy.

The boy's face kept returning to the man's thoughts, the momentary gleam of trust and hope that had been

116

extinguished as he had returned to playing the game. As he dealt again, he wondered about the boy, "Probably just an orphan," he told himself. He continued in his pursuit of happiness, playing the game, eventually forgetting the boy had ever touched him ever so slightly.

And so the man played, neither truly winning nor losing. Always he sat with the same people, or so he thought - at least they had the same look about them, forgetting their faces even as he played. The game grew in importance and he no longer noticed the young child's daily search.

Then one day the little boy didn't come, nor the next day. The man finally noticed the child in his absence. He was quite uncomfortable, feeling guilty until he finally convinced himself that the boy had finally found his "daddy."

Then the boy appeared, much paler and thinner, the eyes pulling, compelling, as the man looked into them. They stared at each other again, much longer this time, but the man pulled himself away and back to the stronger compulsion of the game. The boy continued to stand next to the man in the black suit, but finally he said to himself, "No, you're not my daddy," and slowly he went to the other tables to continue his search.

The man felt him leave, and almost stood up to follow him, but hesitated and returned to his seat as he looked at the money on the table, beckoning him. He reached for the cards as they slid across the table to him. He had lost money that day, too much money. But he would win it back - what he had lost and much more. If not today, then tomorrow, if not then - well, the next day. There would always be a tomorrow, he thought.

"Tomorrow" came, as did the little boy, but the money didn't. The man lost, and lost, even as he told himself he would certainly win the next hand. He tore his suit searching for more money; the more he searched, the more the tears multiplied.

Now he looked just like the other players, mechanical, statues, empty. He played with his jacket off so as to hide the tears. The room seemed to grow hotter as he shed his jacket, as more depended on the fall of the cards. He loosened his necktie, as the room grew even hotter. He finally forgot to shave or even to eat. He never left the table, not even to sleep. The game was ever important.

He won and the money was gone, down the holes in his pockets as he concentrated on the game. He won, but needed much more, much more money.

Throughout this, the boy wandered throughout the room, and finally, again stopped in front of the man, staring, his eyes growing dimmer, as if hope were leaving him. The boy watched as a coin fell from the hole in the man's pocket; he bent down and picked it up, looking at it in wonder at the power it held over the man in front of him. Not understanding, the boy wearily held the coin out to the man as he watched him play the game.

The man had put all his remaining money in the pot. Now he looked and felt like the other players, much as if he had never felt the rain on a gentle summer day, nor wandered through a meadow along gently flowing brook. The man lost - searching his pockets, finding nothing, a look of uncomprehending disbelief growing on his face. No longer sure of the "inevitability" of winning, he had nothing left to hold onto. He found himself staring at the coin being held out to him by the lost child. It shone with an orange glow, reflecting light coming through the

118

window, the boy disappeared from his vision - -the coin, his one last chance!

He grabbed for the coin, finally encountering the eyes of the child again. He tore the coin away, avoiding those eyes, and turned back to the table, to the deadly game. Later, he thought, I'll do something. The game must be won. He did take time to smile a thank you to the child.

The smile that felt very strange; his face had not shown emotion for... for how long? This time he felt chilled as the cards slid across the table to him, chilled-strange in the hot room. His perspiring hands made the cards sticky as he slowly picked them up. He wondered if the others felt this way, chilled inside and yet perspiring in the heat of the room. He looked at them and their usually expressionless faces seemed to take on leering smiles as the betting came around to him. The glow from the window had deepened, and now fell on their faces, adding to their fiendish appearance.

He lifted the one coin to place his bet, and for once he hesitated. If he lost, he'd even kill to get more money to bet with - he'd even sell his soul, though he doubted he had one.

He looked at the faces around him and saw them as if for the first time. One was merely skin and bones, the eyes protruding; another was also just skin and bones, but the eyes sunken, almost nonexistent. Others were swollen hideously, none looked quite human. He couldn't be like them he thought as he pushed the coin to the center of the table; finally seeing his own hand, bent, soaked with perspiration, unlike any hand of his he had ever seen before. He continued to stare at his hand, withdrawing it from the table, still holding the coin. He looked at the faces of his fellow players and felt a revulsion he had not

119

allowed himself to experience before, his gaze traveled slowly, looking for some indication that life existed within, and found only the game reflected back at him, lost, empty and hopeless.

As he turned, he found himself looking into the eyes of the little boy, hopeless, yet hopeful; friendless, yet friendly. The man felt the room grow cooler as their eyes met and held. He felt warmth growing inside, after the corpselike stares of the other players.

The man looked at his cards and then at the child beside him. Slowly, with effort and determination that he had not known he possessed, he threw the cards away from him. His hands felt strangely empty until the boy grasped one, and now the man felt strangely filled. He took the coin and placed it into the child's other hand and slowly left the seat he had occupied for so long.

The game continued without him; another was soon found to take his place. But his man left the game behind him, and he took the child's hand and they walked out of the room together and into the light of the deepening sunrise.

Movement Six - And the Greatest of these is Love

April 2005

Love calls us out of ourselves and into the human family. Somehow, remaining a five-year-old sitting on God's lap was not enough. I needed to learn to love people as well; I wanted to love people as well. But I needed them to show me that they could love me, too. And throughout the course of my healing journey, they did. Countless people have shined their lights into my life at that moment when darkness threatened. Eventually, I started to count on this happening when I needed it.

In Love with God – my story - November 2004

Being in love is hard work, and being in love with God is no different. God often does things or lets things happen which I don't like. And I am sure that I do things that God doesn't like. But the passion that comes from being in love with God fuels me every day. It fuels my writing and my preaching; it even fuels playing with my dogs.

We have this game in my household, called "Get that black dog" in which Dewey and I chase Spirit around the house, grabbing the toy and losing it back to her, chasing her around the house again, all the while disturbing the placement of the rugs with our play.

I am convinced that our sense of humor and our laughter come from being created in the image and likeness of God. Forgetting to play is forgetting to worship part of who God is. Forgetting to laugh dries up a piece of who we are. It is as if I worship that part of God as I run around the house with Dewey and Spirit, getting my rugs all bunched up.

I know that is what we are doing when the congregation laughs at something that I said in my sermon. This laughter brings us closer together, strengthening the bond of love that exists between us. Our humor and laughter water joy just as surely as do our tears. And it is much more enjoyable to do it this way than the other. And just as important, allowing the stream of God' love within us to bubble and gurgle as it flows. Love is the major ingredient in joy.

This being in love with God and God's sense of humor has played an important part in my healing journey. It was this being in love with God which first caused me to reach out to other people, especially those who needed my help. This made me reach a little farther bit by bit than that with which I was comfortable.

I started college majoring in math, but the numbers didn't sparkle as the words on a written page did. English had never been my best subject; but after working on the school newspaper and the literary magazine, I changed majors to English. I again reached farther towards others after I graduated when I decided that I wanted to teach after all. And that was the lure that brought me out to the Indian reservation in South Dakota after I got my teaching certificate. The idea of volunteering my time and energy to help God's people at the Mission school inspired me. It was a way of loving in return the God who so loved me.

The Warmth which Keeps us Going - fiction - 1989

I really did not want to go into work that morning. That week had been the worst in recent memory. I had fought with my boyfriend Bart; my cat had forgotten what kitty litter was for; my van had had a flat and someone had stolen the spare; and my favorite client had fallen and re-broken a few bones while trying to walk for the first time in almost a year. She was back in the same hospital room she had been in before, a room filled with memories of loss.

Paula had been in an auto accident that had claimed the life of two of her three children, and her husband, who had escaped with only a concussion, blamed her somehow for the accident. And he had been driving. She'd been practically crushed, and yet had struggled back in only a year to the threshold of walking again. The specialist wasn't sure how the new breaks would heal. For some reason she listened to the fellow's gloomy predictions this time, and had decided that walking was something that only other people could do. I decided to give that specialist my cat as a "gift."

Someone was, predictably, in my parking spot, and I had to park clear around the block, next to a splintered fence surrounding a gray house with a fallen roof. It took me five minutes to walk back. Bet that's where I lost my tire, the last time I had to park back there. I wouldn't even park Bart there, willingly. Might leave the cat there, though. No, I'd miss him, too, and if he cut his paws I'd be taking him to the vet . . . and I needed to buy new tires.

Paula's gloomy face greeted me when I walked in, the chart said that her husband hadn't visited or called back since we reported the fall to him. Him, I'd park in the space where all the nails from that splintered fence had ended up. Giving him the cat wouldn't be fair to the cat.

Paula had always been saying that Phil would come around, and accept responsibility for the accident. He'd been arguing about something and lost track of where he'd been going. A cement truck, traveling a bit faster than it was supposed to, smashed into the passenger side of the station wagon when he ran the red light. Phil said the argument was all her fault and wouldn't even visit their son Jimmy in the hospital more than once a month.

Jimmy went home to his father after six months later, Paula's still here, and the other two children are buried deep under ground. I hope he at least went to the funerals. Paula couldn't. Until the fall, that was the only thing she had let bother her. That and Joey Winston.

Joey Winston had been my biggest failure until Paula had taken a hand. She couldn't handle his attitude and told him so. He'd had a knee operation, and refused to learn to bend his knee again. He said it hurt too much to try. She kept telling him how she'd show him up, with broken ankles as well as mashed knees. The specialist had kept saying the surgeon should have amputated. She was just as determined to prove him wrong, as she was to show Joey how to do it. They both had to listen as she did what she said - both of her knees were bending before Joey even worked his up halfway. Tired of being needled, Joey got his knee working and is now playing softball.

Joey visited Paula twice as often as her husband Phil did. I tried to think of something appropriate to wish onto Phil, but couldn't come up with anything - and I knew Paula would feel even worse tomorrow, as Phil would have forgotten about their twentieth anniversary that was today. I decided not to wish her a happy anniversary, as that would remind her that Phil had forgotten.

I brought Paula out to exercise the leg that wasn't in a cast, but she wouldn't even acknowledge that I was talking to her. I thought I saw Joey Winston hiding in the bushes, but decided I was imagining things since it was a school day. Why I thought that Joey would think that that meant he should be in school, I don't know.

One of the nurses' aides called and told me Bart was on the phone. I left Paula contemplating our imitation fig tree on the lawn across from the terrace and attended to the argument from the night before. Men are the only thing God shouldn't have created - well, maybe Siamese cats too.

After a short walk of 45 minutes to recover from my phone call, I returned to the terrace and saw Joey Winston doing deep knee bends and, oh, no, he actually did a flip! And ...I hate to think of him injuring his knee again on hospital grounds, but...Paula was paying attention. And beginning to exercise the good knee. Praise God. Now if he would only do something with our respective men.

I chased Joey away after he looked like he was tiring performing his physical display. Paula wasn't her old self, yet she wasn't morose anymore. I left that afternoon, still worried, but hopeful.

When I got to my van, I checked it out carefully, and it was all intact. As I prepared supper, I remembered I had forgotten Bart the boyfriend's birthday present back in my office. I decided to return to claim it.

As I left my office, I heard laughter in Paula's room. Inside were Joey Winston, Jimmy and her husband. A large arrangement of flowers had "Happy Anniversary" on it. Paula's smile threatened to break her face in two. Jimmy and Joey were taking turns doing flips. I left before my foul mood could infect their joy. The present had not been where I had left it. I was looking forward to a stormy evening at home.

Maybe God shouldn't issue a recall on all men, only Italian ones. And all cats, I thought as I walked into my once sweet-smelling apartment. Pussy Foot was being recalcitrant.

After a brief straitening up, my apartment, cat and myself were ready for Bart's birthday supper. I was trying to make believe I was Italian and had cooked some pasta; at least that was what it was supposed to be. Didn't look like any pasta I had ever seen before. Turned out green. I made myself a promise to eat with my eyes closed.

Bell's ringing, Bart' s here, Pussy Foot meowed at me, as if I couldn't tell on my own. Praying for fortitude, I opened the door. Wasn't Bart. Was a bunch of men with banjoes singing some strange songs. Bell rang again, this time I found myself holding a dozen roses. The strange men were still singing. Pussy Foot enjoyed them and tried to help them sing. The neighbors' dogs were doing a much better job.

The third time the bell rang, I was on my way to the garbage to throw out the pasta, which was congealing into a soggy mass of yuck. Finally, Bart was here, and there I was caught red-handed with proof of my marvelous cooking ability. He swept in, grabbed me, the yuck landing on his suit jacket, a piece of clothing I had never seen him in before. And probably never will again. I doubt anyone will ever be seen in that jacket again.

Anyway, Pussy Foot loved the whole thing. Seems he likes green yuck. I guess someone should love everything. I know I love Bart. He proposed that night, yuck-suit and all. He made me promise not to play make-believe Italian. He wanted to be the pasta cooker. I guess everyone has to be good for something. That night when I prayed, I told God that he shouldn't recall men after all, only cats.

I began writing "Lectionary Stuff" my second year in seminary. I would research some of the Lectionary passages for the month (the lectionary is a three year cycle of readings of the Bible), and then write a creative response to that passage. I thought of these as bridges from our culture to that of the particular passage. Several of these follow.

The title for this first one comes from Isaiah 2:5. I remember when my Aunt took me to visit the United Nations when I was in high school. I was impressed with the statue, which illustrated the words from verse 2: "They will beat their swords into plowshares and their spears into pruning hooks." The vision of the world turning to peace has always inspired me.

Lectionary Stuff - December 1989
Come, Let Us Walk in the Light of Yahweh
Isaiah 2:1-5

I keep dreaming, hoping, wishing that time has passed enough for Isaiah's vision to come to pass...But in this world..."They shall not learn war anymore"... the thought seems foreign, for we must replace the learning of war with the learning of something else, of peace, and who dares to teach of peace?

Down the block, the children gather around two bodies fighting, taunting screaming, kicking, they help the combatants fight to prove who is stronger, who is better. One lone young man, Martin, leaves the pack, dreaming of other things.

The young women gather, gossiping, cutting down those who try to be different - yet a few leave, dreaming.

Theresa goes off to Calcutta, another woman studies to be a doctor, another to be a minister, all dreaming.

Old men gather, speaking of the coming doom, boasting of glorious deeds past, medals won, foes destroyed. One unnoticed soldier leaves, visits a poor woman, hugs her child while the woman goes off to work to feed the child, all three dreaming.

Dreaming of peace, of walls destroyed which seemed would be there forever - the Berlin wall, the wall between the east and west, the walls between neighbors.

Who dares to teach of peace?

May We Abound in Hope - 1990
Romans 15:4-13

Lost, I wander
Once - I knew...
knew much of God, of glory sung
by prophets of old.
But now - lost, I wander.

Wander within
within the sanctuary
hoping.
Hoping to find welcome
oneness
Christ personified
with spirit
sharing.

Hoping to be found
again.

Welcome greets me
as once I greeted
others.
Christ's love heals me
as once I helped
heal others.
God's arms find me
holding close.

And I learn to sing
again.

1 Corinthians 13 is that poem to love that is often read at both weddings and funerals. It describes the wonder of the fullness of God's love - a fullness for which Paul, while writing the letter, yearned. But his letter was written to a church that was split into factions, factions that Paul wanted to stop arguing as to which was the most important. Paul clearly stated in this that no matter what we may do, if we do not do it in love, it is worth nothing. In the midst of the conflict, Paul yearned for the love he himself had experienced in his vision from God, an experience that he likened looking into a metal pot lid (our equivalent of the mirror of his day) compared to what he expected when he experienced the resurrection. For Paul in this letter of First Corinthians, what matters most is how fully we love each other. And so we use his love poem when we need to be reminded of the wonder of love the most - at weddings and funerals.

Noise - May 1990
1 Corinthians 13

Empty noise fills the summer's day.
A politician running for office
A psychic selling the future,
A pastor speaking of faith with a stone heart
A millionaire, with guilt guiding his way,
giving millions to the poor he'd broken.

Empty noise filling the moonlit night.
Just met lovers promising fidelity
until tomorrow.

Empty noise.

An unnoticed woman, poor and tattered,
walking through the park
patiently searching, finally catching,
a wayward puppy long lost.
Not her pet, but for the child next door.
A quiet "thank you" worth all the trouble.

Two old people, one man, one woman,
sit together quietly under the moon.
Smile and whisper together of times
they'd left, but come back to hug and heal
of times spanning half the century –
times of crying, times of rejoicing.

Empty noise and quiet strength
go hand and hand it seems.
Yet those who look upon the other
with eyes of knowledge and wisdom,
those eyes shall see God face to face.

To Know and Be Known - 1990
I Corinthians 13

Lord, I tremble
when I think of what I have not done,
of the stranger I have not welcomed
of the stranger's customs I've refused to learn
Holding proudly to my own heritage,
boasting, puffed-up, a law unto myself.

Lord, I tremble
when I remember what I have done,
the friend I was too hurried to wait for
the ones I've quarreled with, ignored,
filling my own stomach first,
not worrying who may be hungry or hurt.

Lord, I tremble
in fear, yes, for I have felt your love,
have felt your love enfold me, heal me.
I know my own shortcomings stop me,
hold me back, here on earth
I do not love, do not reach out, as I ought.

Lord, I tremble
in hope and faith, as I turn my eyes
to another center, as I move my thoughts
from focusing within to focusing without.
No longer counting by how far I get
but by the friends I wait for
wait with as they hunger and fear.
Now, building up through the power of love.

Lord, I tremble
in anticipation, as I strive to know,
those around me, as I reach out, not in,
I look to the time when my knowledge fills
knowing even you, my Lord,
as fully as I am known by you.

Tale of a Woman - fiction - 2005
from John 4

It was so hard to come out to this well, to carry back the water she needed to live. If she went when the day was cool, the others would spill her water more often than not. They liked to imagine how much better they were – and loved to jostle her when she was almost home while the other women smiled encouragingly to remind themselves how lowly she was compared to them. Without the water, she would die – so to the well she went. And this day, as every day at this time, it was much too hot to carry a heavy jug.

Wait – a man was sitting on the edge of the well – how could she approach – how could she not, for the day was hot and there was no water at home, she could not afford to be thrown out again.   But he was dressed as a rabbi, a Jew – a Jew that would hate her even more than the other women did; he would hate a Samaritan, perhaps throw her down the well. How could she approach – but how could she not? Perhaps if she didn't look at him it would work, how could he be offended if she didn't look at him? But with a Jew, her just being alive could offend him. But it was so hot and dry. . . Perhaps his eyes would not see someone as lowly as herself.

"Will you give me a drink?"

The voice was kind, but the woman was filled with terror. A Jew was speaking to her; if she replied, he might kill her. If she didn't, he most certainly would. "You are a Jew and I am a Samaritan woman. How can you ask me for a drink?" Her limbs could not hold still as she replied. If there had been water in the jug, none would remain.

"If you knew who I am, you would be asking me for a drink, and I would give you fresh, living water."

Fresh, living water - she almost didn't remember what it tasted like. She hadn't even seen fresh, living water since her third husband had thrown her out of the house for not bearing him a son. The idea of drinking water that she didn't have to strain before drinking, water that didn't taste of the stone of the well – that was just a dream. "Are you a better man than our ancestor who dug this well?"

"Everyone who drinks this water will be thirsty again, but whoever drinks the water I will give him will never thirst."

This man was crazy, but not threatening. He was speaking to her kindly, something that had not happened in years, anyone speaking to her kindly, but a man . . . crazy, yes, but the sound of his voice had something new within it, something she had never heard before. A sense of peace settled over her. "Sir, give me this water."

"Go, call your husband, and come back."

The sense of peace disappeared, replaced with one of self-loathing. "I have no husband."

"You are speaking truly, in fact you have had five husbands."

The voice was still kind as it told of the facts of her life. The eyes that looked into hers were filled with love, instead of hate. "Sir, I can see you are a prophet." Her voice shook as she spoke, even more than her limbs had before, whether with fear or with hope, she truly had no idea.

And so they spoke, this Samaritan woman and the Jewish rabbi. A cold, iciness that had permeated her heart melted. She began to accept whom she had become, as a person worthy of living, and perhaps, being loved.

Rigidness, placed within her body by fear so slowly over the years that she had not noticed, disappeared under the man's steady gaze. And he told her that he was the Messiah, and she knew with all her being that he was telling the truth. This man was not crazy. Warmth flooded her heart, light filled her body.

This gift this man gave her was too marvelous to keep to herself. It was even too marvelous to keep from those who had spent many years persecuting her so that they could feel worthy. She felt that she must share it with those who had but the day before spit on her in the marketplace; she felt she must share this vision of joy and love, of peace and worthiness. She felt that she had to run so they could come before he left on his way . . .

And those to whom she spoke saw the change within her being, and ran to the well and also spoke to the Christ. Love sparkled in the life of that town from that day forward.

Hands that Reach Out - my story - 2005

I probably would still be hiding in the darkness if people had not reached out to me, embodying Christ's love to me. I knew that Jesus loved me as I sat on his lap in heaven – at least the five year old me knew that. But the part of me that lived on earth with everybody else wasn't that sure – of anything.

My shell cracked when my mother died and the memories began to return. Many people around me reached their hands into the shell, ignoring its sharp edges. Their hands touched mine, and I began to emerge, to give birth to myself. One Methodist prayer group removed much of the shell as they accepted me as one of their own. I know that someone in that prayer group prayed at ten o'clock at night, prayed for me at ten o'clock at night, because I felt a sense of peace and wholeness at that time. I felt this almost every night.

People were there when I needed them. Their love called out to that river within me that had become frozen. And slowly that river thawed. And slowly that river flowed. And now it flows as freely as any river, dancing over the rocks towards the source of life.

"We Love Him Because He First Loved Us" – meditation - April 2005

Do we really know what love is until we experience divine love? I think not. Human love is based on so many conditional things. Yes, when we are first born our parents often do feel unconditional love for us. But then we need our diapers changed in the middle of the night. Then we need much care when we catch those inevitable colds of childhood. We are no longer cute when our nose is running.

Later in our experience of human love, we try to find that spouse who will be successful, that spouse who will help us – or perhaps that spouse whom we can rescue and thereby fulfill our own need to be needed. When the spouse doesn't succeed or one of the couple becomes healthy and doesn't need the other in the same way, he or she no longer need rescuing, love can wither.

God's love does not wither when our noses are runny, or when we fail, or when we no longer need to be propped up to function. God's love comes with no conditions, not even those conditions listed in the Ten Commandments. However often we break those Ten Commandments, God's love is still present, waiting for us to access it. We close ourselves off to it; God does not turn it off to us. That living water is always there and waiting for any who are thirsty to drink.

We turn ourselves off to it because it changes us. It causes us to laugh more; it causes us to love more – and we don't always appreciate laughter and love is sometimes inconvenient as it makes us vulnerable to hurt and loss. We can stay in that crab shell our whole lives and never experience – truly – divine or human love.

God's love only strengthens as we allow it into our lives. And when we do that, we begin to understand what love really is all about. It is that love that allows us to dance when we are tired, that allows us to rejoice with our friends when we have no reason to rejoice for ourselves. It is that love that we can depend upon to be there when we need it

Once we open to divine love, we learn how to love in return. We love God in return; we celebrate the presence of God's love in our lives by loving other people, by helping other people. We also come to accept and celebrate who we are, as unique children of God. The poor and the hungry truly become our brothers and sisters because we love them as fellow children of God. We are able to love them because we have also learned to love ourselves. It becomes harder to walk by someone who has fallen to the ground without stopping to help them up. It becomes easier to accept the hand that reaches out to help us up when we have fallen.

Our heart becomes as God's heart – but not quite. We never, really, make it to fully embodying the love that Christ has for all. But that is as it is supposed to be. Accepting our limitations is but one step in learning to "do justice, love mercy and walk humbly with our God."[4]

---

[4] Micah 6:8

(If Ruth had been a reasonable member of her culture she would have sent her mother-in-law back to her own land, refusing to desert Naomi when both their husbands had died was definitely not to her best interests. Had she stayed in her father's house in her own land, she could have married again. A woman, two women alone in Israel of that time were of no significance, little value in the scheme of things. But Ruth did not want Naomi to go back alone into obscurity and poverty. Ruth gave up much of her own chance at life -by herself Naomi in Israel would have none. Ruth took a chance out of love. God blessed them both as Ruth found a husband - and became an ancestor of Jesus of Nazareth.)

October 1990
You will not Return Alone -
Ruth 1:1-19a

Times of darkness come
The Lord's promise seems gone
The hand of God appears to smite
rather than to heal, to punish
rather than to bless.

Hope seems empty
as we turn homewards.
Bitterness beckons
for we have been faithful -
where is the Lord who loves?

Yet the promise
travels with us.
We are not alone.
A companion gives strength.
And we travel homeward
hoping in the promise.

Hoping the rains which threaten
feed the lands
hoping the storm clouds lighten,
to show the sun,
hoping that once again
the promise will flower
and joy will fill our hearts
once again.

Love thy Neighbor - 1990
Mat. 22:34-46

Love the Lord with all thy heart
and the Lord's love will flow
into thy heart -
healing the pain
soothing the sorrow,
teaching love, changing,
showing the value of others -
others to love and cherish.
Precious gifts.
Opportunities to love,
allowing the Lord's love
to flow more fully
changing, until we love
even ourselves.

Gifting the Joy - my story - December 2004

I think that the reason I became a pastor was so that I could share what I can of the love that I have experienced, both from God and from others. I find that it is in the sharing of this that I experience joy more fully. What I love most is preaching.

My most vivid memory of preaching comes from when I was still in seminary. It was my task to preach to my home church the Sunday before Desert Shield became Desert Storm. Using my experience as a high school English teacher, I tried to have something for everyone in the sermon as much as I could. And for this sermon, I had two called-up reservists, one a nurse, as well as my pastor in the congregation. Joe was well known for appearing on TV for protesting outside the local GE munitions plant. The next day, he planned to lead a Martin Luther King Day prayer service with one of the Berrigan brothers, a well-known Roman Catholic peace activist.

I preached that we each have a call. Some risk their lives to protect others. Others to make sure those leaders who have access to big sticks (our military) don't get carried away using them and waste them, breaking them unnecessarily, and breaking others as well. As you might guess, I have pacifist tendencies, but would not pass muster as a Quaker pacifist. I am still somewhat aggressive, as anyone who has played cards with me knows.

The next day, Joe repeated much of what I said, asking those who had military in their family serving in the Gulf to stand up. Joe stated that "our prayers go with them," but they have their call and "we have ours". This was the first time I have heard myself quoted, and that gave strength to my desire to give everyone a piece of God's love whenever possible.

We each have a call, our very own call that changes at different points in our lives. When we follow that road, our lives contain the most joy. It is not an easy road, but it is the most fulfilling. And we have help getting over the obstacles when we need it.

We can and do experience a taste of the resurrection here and now in the healing which we allow God's spirit to perform in our lives. That Spirit will not grab hold of us and demand that we accept its presence in our lives. But when we allow it to enter our lives, our lives are changed. We experience that taste of the resurrection that is available here and now.

It is something that we share when we share the stories of faith that we have experienced in our lives. The theme of resurrection has filled the Good News, which I share with those around me. The presence of God's spirit in the world is a gift, which is available to all, no matter what name they may give to the divine. It is a gift, nothing needs to be done in order to earn it; but it causes transformation in all who allow it to enter their lives. This taste of the resurrection is but a taste of the love that God has for all of us.

Movement Seven - Joy - a Taste of the Resurrection

Joy gives us a taste here and now of what the resurrection will be like. Joy places little jewels in our paths that we can see if we stay aware of their presence. For me, it is the moments of joy that make life worth living; those moments when we experience a closeness to God that reminds us of our status as God's children, as God's beloved children. The sparkling diamonds of joy can turn even the deepest darkness into a time of rejoicing, lighting our way along our path.

The Magic of Holy Week - my story - 2005

The fullness of joy rarely comes without an experience of darkness. It is as if we cannot get to Easter Sunday without going through Good Friday. Just as childbirth requires labor, so, too, does the experience of the fullness of joy. The sparkles of joy can hit us at any time. Sparkles caused just by the smile of a stranger can transform our day, just as one of our smiles can change someone else's. But the fullness of joy is something else.

I have felt this fullness of joy when pieces of myself have returned; on days such as that one described in my poem "And I Shall Dance this Way Again," days such as that intense attack of spring fever when for the first time I stopped expecting someone to jump out from behind a bush to attack me, days such as the one that being touched first felt good. For each one of these days, the light that has filled my life has changed and gotten brighter. My smile has made a greater impact on the world around me as I allow it to become a greater part of my life.

There exists in my heart an almost constant warmth, an assurance that life has more to gift me with, an assurance that telling my story will add to the sparkles of joy that dance around in this world, joy that can enter into someone else's darkness. An assurance that, if I share my light, someone will find the sun rising on their dark highway just a little bit sooner.

I am different after having written this book. My life has become brighter as I have spoken about the darkness in which I lived, in which many of us live. But God is there to hold all of us; all of us have a place saved for us within the divine heart. If I can find God under a bed, where in your life might you find that same love?

148

Joy – meditation - January 2005

We ask God for many things, for world peace, for health for a loved one, for a promotion at work, for many things, which, we think, will make our lives better. God has promised that our prayers will be answered. But we often don't get that better job, our loved one dies, and world peace seems farther away than ever. Unhappiness increases around us.

But God does not promise happiness, the possession of things that make us contented. God gives us what we need when we pray. We get the unsettled spirit which leads us to seek out another company for which to work, or perhaps another, more fulfilling career entirely. We are filled with a sense of peace in spite of our loss as our loved one's suffering ends. And, most importantly, we are changed as we pray for peace. We become someone who truly values peace, filled with a willingness to struggle to work toward it.

As we continue to pray, we become filled with a light, a sense of God's love filling us in response. One day, that sense becomes joy, the light of God's presence residing in our hearts. Joy is much better than happiness. Happiness is a state of having, joy is a state of being. As we continue to allow God's love to transform us, joy becomes a habit. A habit which allows us to be assured of God's love in the midst of unemployment, in the midst of deep bereavement, in the midst of devastating war. This joy is a taste of the promise of the resurrection which God has given to us, a promise much more valuable than even world peace. A promise that is given to all along with the gift of life itself.

149

Joy is what provides light in whatever valley of the shadow of death we might find ourselves traveling. God did not promise we would never travel in that valley, but God does promise a light to lead us out again. When we arrive on the other side, we are not the same person as when we started. We carry the light dancing within ourselves.

Rainbows and Tears - 1989

A mist covered gray day
surrounds my life and dreams.
A smoke-filled, jet black night
enfolds my hopes and my soul.
I see my life
but black and gray
charred, once-living trees
fencing all without.

What hope do I of else?
A question asked, a question burned,
a question torturing thought.
I close my eyes and hope of more
I trust and love
I dream and hope.

A touch of love
unnoticed first
yet felled the darkened walls.

The black comes light
Filled blue, filled green, filled red.
The gray comes life
filled green, orange, yellow bright.

Love enfolds all with growth as
the day bursts forth and colors fill
the eyes of those around.
The night lacks fear now brings
peace, souls find joy
encased in a stream of love.

The pain still grabs
but loses hold.
The ash but accents
a rainbow stream
flowing through
within, without, all around.

I open my eyes
still pain, still ash
but yet now joy
from deep inside myself.

A light bright enfolds my world
showering rainbows throughout
bought through His sacrifice
and the courage of my tears.

Bashful and the Gypsy - fiction - 1989

Bashful'd been without a woman for the last 273 years, a short time really, but life did get boring after awhile. He tried dating a few times, but he couldn't seem to find a woman to put that zing in his step. No matter what, he still found himself plodding along, dreaming of finding her some day.

Her... what would she be like? Certainly not like the tooth fairy. That woman wasn't pleased with any man. Bashful dated her a few times, had been promised anything he desired, the tooth fairy liked to show off her magic wand. She only did it, though, when she was pleased with him, and after displeasing her three days in a row, he gave up. Bashful didn't care for dishes coming out of thin air aiming at his head. Dishes and ice cubes and cats. Dangerous woman to be around that tooth fairy was.

The woman that would put zing in his step wouldn't be like the nymph either. Bashful had almost been lovesick staring at her reflection in the water. The nymph held the beauty of the stars in her eyes, the sun flowed from her smile, and her hair resembled a golden waterfall. But whenever he had tried to touch, to hold, his hand broke the water surface and the nymph fled. She couldn't handle the warmth he had to give; she was too frozen, lifeless. Just an image really.

Bashful wanted a woman with substance, not physical substance, but a more magical, spiritual quality which showed she wanted to be alive, to experience what life has to offer and to offer much back to life. Most of the other dwarves turned up with superficial women. The only woman he admired, Snow White, was so fully in love with her prince that only friendship was left for him.

Well, that friendship was enough for now, he thought as he mused trying to decide what to give her for her birthday. He'd skipped the last twelve birthday parties, feeling sorry for himself and alone, but he'd had enough of that. Just because he couldn't find a woman to believe in his magic, he didn't have to stop believing in himself.

He went into his workshop and surveyed his domain. None of the other dwarves dared come in this room - open the wrong drawer and buzzards fly out, or a grizzly bear roar would deafen you, or who knows what. But he knew this room. He wasn't scared in the least, he'd tamed most of the demons within, and now they worked as a source of creative power for him. Strange thing about demons, they hold so much energy, but it doesn't have to destroy. Aim it right and you've got some of the most beautiful stuff around.

He chose a drawer, opened it, and took out a glob of black goo. Out of another he took green slime and 2 nightmares. His pile didn't quite please him, so he added a pound of blue bile. He mixed it in a large bowl and poured it into what appeared to be a portable typewriter, except it wasn't, as typewriters hadn't been invented yet. The combined gloop gurgled and spun and disappeared with not a speck to be seen. Bashful hit a few keys, mumbling, "the quick brown fox jumped over the gray dog," a very powerful incantation, if you know anything about spells.

A fog appeared in the corner, and slowly from it emerged a rainbow green star quilt, with an eagle majestically imposed onto the center. The star radiated rainbows out in six directions, the eagle looked right in your eyes and you felt yourself freely soaring over a cliff in gorgeous snow capped mountains that...

Well, anyway, out of that gloop, Bashful made a quilt like none other seen before. Content that he had created an appropriate gift, he boxed and wrapped the quilt - after inventing boxes and birthday wrapping paper.

Bashful traveled by himself to the party as the other dwarves had left the house early to pick up their girls. There was a bet among them as to whose date was the most beautiful, and they all wanted to make sure their dates all had on their best fancy clothes.

Unfortunately, he didn't have a lamp to use. Grumpy had taken two as the last time he'd been out on a date, the woman had complained all evening about not being able to see on the way and stubbing her toe six or seven times.

As he neared the bridge across Wishing Creek, the moon disappeared behind dark storm-like clouds. Bashful decided to hurry as he forgot to make his box waterproof. He started to run and ran smack into...someone, and tumbled into the creek, both of them ended up in the goop. Fortunately, he dropped the box onto the bridge deck as he fell.

The box was nice and dry, but he sure wasn't. Water dripped off his nose, his hair resembled wet spaghetti after you soak it for three days and...

Bashful looked again at the person across from him. He wished he'd seen those eyes before so he could have used them as models for his eagle's eyes for that picture he was painting, he'd never...

The rainbow star wasn't brighter than that woman's smile...woman? Oh no, where were his manners? Bashful began to apologize profusely, but only "I'm" came out of his mouth. The other words got stuck behind his tonsils.

Never had the nymph's smile held him thus. And this was a real person, not an image...He thought as he reached out to touch to make sure. A very wet person, he confirmed.

He looked up at the gift, dry on the bridge. Looking away from those eyes enabled his words to escape, and he offered the apparition of beauty use of the quilt for warmth. An offer gratefully accepted, with an apology - the essence of beauty before him thought that it was her fault!

To make a long story short, the lady he had knocked off the bridge was Snow White's second cousin, whom she had invited with him, Bashful, in mind. They hit it off well after they both dried off a bit.

Doc won the prize for the most beautiful date. At first, Bashful was furious that his lady didn't win, but he didn't mind after awhile that no one else saw her beauty the way he did...because no one else saw his magic quite the way she did either.

That Taste that leaves us Dancing - my story - January 2006

I really don't know how to describe that feeling that occurs when I leave a place of darkness, even if it is just physical darkness, and move into the light except to say that my spirit dances. When the sun breaks out on a rainy day, my spirit dances. When sadness leaves and light returns, my spirit dances.

I truly believe that what of this that we experience here and now is but a taste of what is to come. Perhaps it is just the smell of the appetizer that is the prelude to the grandest banquet of which we ever partake. It is not a coincidence that the great wedding banquet shows up several times in the Gospels.

We can dance through life or we can stumble. With our faces forever looking down we will not see the light. Dancing around, filled with life, we can spend our life celebrating Christmas and moving towards Easter instead.

I have chosen to dance.

Living Water – prose poem – April, 2005
from John 4 - dancing version

I thirst, but nothing seems to ease my thirst. I thirst, but the water from the well does not last long as it flows down my throat. An hour later, I thirst again. I yearn for a drink that will fill the hole in my heart, a drink that will sustain the life within me.

I thirst, and I reach out to the well – but someone is there before me. How can I fill my needs with this man blocking my way? A man who would just as soon throw me down the well as allow me access to the water, a man who would despise me because of who I was born to be, someone not like him, someone without privilege . . . and this man asks me for water.

I thirst, but I am safe for now. I will give him his water and perhaps he will leave. Perhaps he will then move on and I will be able to slake my own thirst – for a moment. I ask him how he, a Jew, could ask me, a Samaritan woman for a drink, to make sure this is not a trick, a trick to catch me and then punish me. I look forward to my own drink . . . and this man, this Jew who should hate me offers me living water . . . such water as I have not had in years, water clean, water pure . . . and then he offers me water more filling than living water. I accept his offer and look into his eyes.

What I see amazes me. The love in his eyes, love for me, is more brilliant than the love had been in my mother's eyes so many years ago when I presented her with a gift of living water as a child. The love in his eyes, for me, is more brilliant than the love my first two husbands looked at me with before I was unable to give them the sons they needed to carry on their family name. The love in his eyes is more brilliant than the brightest sun I have ever seen on a clear morning after that rain that gives us the living water finishes blessing the earth.

Some hole in my heart is mended. Some fear in my heart is defeated. I no longer see myself as a five times divorced Samaritan woman whose value the world despises. The value of my life is held in the gaze of this man's eyes. I am filled with an intense need to share what I have been given, and so I run. I run to the houses of those who mocked me but yesterday. I share with them the news of this man's eyes, how they see not a Samaritan, but a beloved friend. I run to the houses of those who banished me from their list of friends and share with them the news of the living water of love that could be theirs if they just let down their guard.

And they listen. They run to the water and the man gazes at them as well, the holes in their hearts are also healed. The look of fear that comes into their eyes with the approach of any Jew flees, and doesn't return even when the man's followers question his actions. We rejoice when he stays with us a few days. No more time is needed for our lives to be transformed. In truth, that one look was all that was necessary.

The marvelous thing about allowing God's love in, to flow through our hearts and out into the world is that the more we do this the more it stays inside our own heart. The more we love others the more our hearts sparkle with joy. The more we brighten the days of others, the brighter the sun shines in ours. The more we help others travel through their dark night of the soul, the easier it is to travel through our own – for we have the memories of what we shared with them as well as their helping hands as we travel over the rocky chasm and into the sunlight once more.

God's love is like diamonds sparkling at midnight and is even more durable. May the treasure of God's love fill your heart this day.

Dancing in the Daylight - prose poem - 2005

Lord, I forget why I was dancing yesterday afternoon. The sky is just as clear as it was then. The birds fill the leaves with song as the wind brushes through them. The trees offer shade and protection from the strength of the sun, and that sun is shining just as brightly. Why was I dancing as if the world would be shaken loose from its moorings?

My heart is as light as it was then. My life is as filled with the presence of love. I look before me and I look behind me and I see the presence of light filling my life. What was there different about yesterday that my heart was so filled that my body could not stay still?

I don't want to remember the darkness of yesterday morning. I don't want to remember the darkness that held my heart so tightly in its grip. But – I do remember. And when I remember the darkness, I begin, again, to dance in the daylight.

November 2004

Life is a cyclic journey, as we move through periods of growth and periods of lying fallow. We often follow the same pattern, growing and risking, experiencing hurt, allowing the presence of God's love to heal us, and then taking the risk of reaching out and growing one more time. The following poem reprises the story that I have shared with you.

A Desert of Silence - 1989

Silence surrounding the child
echo less vacuum, desert dry world
frozen, no brightness.
Sitting, eyes closed, mind shut
speaking within to One who listens.

Listening herself, for love that comes
surrounds, makes light
teaching integrity
wholeness.

Outside - chaos, pain, owned guilt
used object
discarded.
Inside peace, warmth, forgiveness
beloved being
treasured.

Seeds of trust
planted, grow
watered in spite of wounds
by wounds healing.

Universe transforming
slowly unfolding
newness surprising
yet always was there
smothered by hate.

Seeds of self
hidden grow
watered by moments of oneness
being of people.

Universe transforming
rapidly growing
lightness surprising
yet new, yet more
self hidden
recovered.
Seeds of openness
planted grow
watered in spite of pain
by pain.

Universe transforming
rainbows bursting
enlightening others
yet always remembering
what was, might still have been.

Seeds of life
unfolding grow
watered by sharing, giving,
dancing duets.

Surprised by self
affirmed by others
standing, speaking, shouting.
Strength, uniqueness echoed back
by a world rainbowed with wonder
filled with beings clothed in uniqueness
filled with a future dreams can not tell.
Dancing alone, yet encircled
Dancing together yet as one.
Dancing with the ones
who listen.

Re-learning to Love Myself – my story
– April 2005

The cyclic and rhythmic nature of my healing journey really stands out. I didn't love myself when I began. Stuff came up and I hated myself. As I dealt with it, I learned to like myself. At that point, stuff came up again. I learned to like myself - just a bit more, and then MORE stuff came up. Then I learned to almost love myself, stuff came up and . . . and today, today I love my self. I can accept that I am truly a child of God, and well loved. Of course, tomorrow I may dislike myself again with more stuff having come up, but then - at this point at least - I know that I will love my self even more than I do today after a bit of work.

I don't remember at what point that I began to really understand the New Testament commandment to "love your neighbor as yourself." It took several cycles before I could accept the fact that I was actually SUPPOSED to love - myself. In the beginning, I didn't think that I mattered at all, I thought that all that mattered was to help God heal God's people - no matter what state I was in myself. But - today - I know that my welfare matters deeply to God.

There was much love at the beginning of my journey between God and myself. And then - as I began healing - God's people reached out to me. As I began to count on this love, I began to reach out in return. Not as I had before when I was being the co-dependent rescuer with no sense of self. Not as I had before with no care as to my own health. I began to realize that only a healthy me could truly love others. I began to realize that I could only love other people to the extent that I also loved myself, that I could only love other people to the extent that I allowed God's love to flow through me. There is a big difference in the amount of love your heart can hold when you allow other people into it.

The difference between the love of God and just me, and the love that allows the presence of others is the difference between static electricity and current electricity. The essence of that flowing energy is joy.

God promises joy - if we allow the presence of God's love into our lives. And more fully as we allow God's love to flow through us and into those around. Then the river of love is more firmly placed in the channel of our hearts. As we give away that energy, we keep the joy.

Many people get confused between joy and happiness. Happiness is a good thing too - but it is tied into doing, rather than being; into having, rather than sharing. People look at others who are happy and want what they see. They want the house by the ocean; they want the car that goes so much faster than the others. But then the big wave comes and the house disappears . . . and the car blows its engine . . . . and all our possessions lose their luster after we have to pack up and move yet again, and again. Happiness only lasts as long as you possess that which has caused the happiness. Happiness only lasts as long as those possessions are fresh and new.

Joy is constantly new as it peeks into our lives. It is always there, hiding around the corner waiting to surprise us.

God does not promise happiness. God does promise the joy that comes with loving others, that joy that comes with shedding light onto another's path when they are lost in the darkness. It is this joy that fills me on Sunday mornings when I get up into the pulpit to preach.

It is this joy that gives us a taste of the resurrection here and now, a taste which God wants to shower on all people.

Postlude

My previous church was in Rensselaer, New York, across the Hudson from Albany. Several members of my congregation had been working in New York City on September 11, 2001. While the Hudson Mohawk Association of which my church and I were members did not include the city, we were affected by the events of that day. My immediate response was to organize an ecumenical prayer service. We had one on that day and another the Friday afterwards when President Bush called for a National Day of Prayer.

At the second service, one member of the congregation told his story. On that day, the people of New York City were transformed from a city of strangers afraid of each other into a family that worked together. He told of a passing parade of bucket loaders that had left their construction site to respond to the emergency. He told a story of people helping each other, supporting each other. The only reason he managed to get home was due to a ride offered by a stranger to the first train station that was still working on the Albany to New York run, a 20-minute ride. That stranger was doing this as her part as service to her fellow New Yorkers, and she had been doing it for some time before she offered this particular ride. Her rides were being gratefully accepted by footsore New Yorkers, a ride that a wise person would not have accepted only hours before.

After those events, I wrote the following letter in my role as President of the local ecumenical group.

A Letter

September 16, 2001

Greetings in Christ:

We, as a people, as a community, have been grievously injured. Our sense of safety, of who we are in this world has been shaken. We are shocked, confused and afraid.

"Where is God?", we ask. And we see answers to this question in the volunteers who have flooded Manhattan. Steel workers, construction workers, and volunteer firemen from other parts of New York, from neighboring states and even from the Midwest. We see the answer in the Teddy Bears, which Oklahoma City is sending to New York City school children - returning the care and concern, which New York gave them after their own catastrophe.

We are like the disciples, locked in a room, afraid for their lives, on that morning we call Easter. We, who call ourselves Christian, know what comes with Easter sunrise.

We are also filled with anger at the cancer of evil that destroyed so much of what we hold dear. We want to destroy that which has destroyed. This is good, because it shows we love, it shows we care. But, it holds a danger, in that we could become like those we despise. If we are not careful, we could become like "them."

We ask God why did this happen, how could the Lord of the universe allow this evil to overtake us? As I go

168

through the "angry at God" phase in my own life, studying the Book of Job helps me. Job cried out in pain at his unmerited suffering, at the unmerited suffering of his family. At first, he expressed his deep faith, then his anger as his troubles threatened to overwhelm him. My search revealed that Christ's answer to Job's cry of pain and anger was to travel down the road to Jerusalem and on to Calvary. Jesus did not turn back once he realized the hatred awaiting him there. How could I continue to be angry with the one who loves me so?

The story did not end, does not end, on that hill so long ago. Easter morning became Easter evening, and fifty days later, Pentecost - when those who had been afraid were so filled with the spirit of God that they went out into the crowds and shared the Good News of the resurrection.

Our police, firemen and EMT's who died did not turn back either. For love of neighbor was stronger than their fear for their own safety. They have received that gift of resurrection.

Evil can only be truly defeated by love. It becomes uncomfortable, and either leaves or is transformed through the power of God's love into something good. We need to use the energy of our anger to say "NO" to hatred, "NO" to violence, and "YES" to the risk of loving those around us. "NO" to vengeance, to becoming like "them," where our rage destroys innocence. "YES" to listening to God's call upon our lives. "YES" to justice, to commitment to a world where children are born and live full lives. "They" were willing to sacrifice their lives for the cause of hatred and violence. What are we, as Christians, as Americans, willing to sacrifice for the sake of Christ, for the sake of God?

Life will return to a "new normal," not to the way it was before September 11, 2001. Our life as a people is at stake in how we respond to this challenge. Do we hear the call of anger and hatred - the same call that "they" who did this heard? Or do we hear the call of Christ?

It is my prayer that the call to which we listen will be the call of Christ. And there are signs that this will be so. 700,000 Americans donated blood in the first 6 hours after the planes struck the towers. The Red Cross went from a shortage which caused hospitals to cancel elective surgery to saying we have all we can handle this week, come back next week to give the gift of life to your fellow Americans.

We hold the gift of life in our hands. Our Lord is calling upon us to give it away, even to those who would do such things as this. It is only by giving this gift away that life around us is transformed. It is only by giving this gift away that we can keep it within our hearts. This violent act will change us forever. With the help of Christ, it will be change for the good.

May the peace of Christ be with you all,
Kathleen Chesnut
President, East Greenbush Cooperative Ministries

The Journey Onward - 2006

I felt anger on September 11, 2001, but I didn't feel the fear that others felt – not really. I knew people were afraid, because they said so. They said that their sense of security had been destroyed through that violence. Evil was something they had rarely thought of until that day, but they thought of little else immediately after the attack. By that day, I had already known the fear of which they were speaking that happens when the foundations of your personal world are shattered; this happened to me when I was five, not in 2001.

In 2001, I already knew the depths to which those who embrace darkness can sink; the intentional destruction of life on that day was nothing new to me. What was new – and what blew my mind – was the fact that so many people ran into those burning buildings at the risk – no, at the cost of their own lives. What was new was that so many others cared about the welfare of strangers. That was what was new. The fear that many people felt was the fear that had started to leave my life on that day of spring fever 20 years ago; echoes of the fear returned in 2001, but anger was my primary response.

I had accepted that there were a few people who accepted God's call to love their neighbors. I had experienced that love. But the sacrifice of the fire fighters, police and other professionals blew my mind, and broke down much of the shielding I had erected to protect myself from others. With their sacrifice and the outpouring of love in response to their sacrifice, I allowed myself to open up more fully.

That outpouring of love and concern that filled our country amazed me. I have a vivid memory of signs on the New York Thruway, hundreds of miles from New York City, telling trucks filled with donations how to find distribution points for their gifts. New York City has itself changed. A minister friend of mine from Chicago brought her youth group to a service project in New York City, and spoke to a homeless man. She had grown up in New York State and wondered how that event had changed things. The man replied that strangers cared for each other now. He reflected on how the homeless people who had lived in the collapsed subway had not been counted in the total of lost lives and how their stories were never told. New York city's homeless were now determined to know each other so people's stories would not be lost. They were now more of a community than a group of strangers.

The entire state has grown closer. Upstate, where I served, and "the city", thought of each other as "us" and "them", groups with little in common. As one member of my congregation expressed it, "we learned they were us."

Unfortunately, that response of love has largely disappeared, and the response of fear has increased. The lesson that "they are us" is one that we have yet to learn. Fear, not love, fills our airwaves now. Fear filled the coverage of our election November of 2004.

And fear destroys love. Allowing fear to rule is not a fitting memorial to those who gave their lives in the hope that someone else might live. Fear belongs to the darkness that destroys, and not the light of love that creates and heals.

The response of love on that day of September 11, 2001, by those who gave their lives and those who allowed strangers to become neighbors compels me to share my story of fear and healing, a story, which says, we do not have to live in a world of fear and darkness. God's light, however you may have been taught of God, is there to guide all of us; God's love is there to heal us and to lead us all through transformation. When we hold God's hand and walk through the curtain of our fears, we enter into a valley filled with the presence of love. And in that valley, whether it is surrounded by the shadow of darkness or by light filled spaces, we experience a taste of the resurrection, the greatest gift that life can give, the fruit of God's love for us.

This book draws to a close, but the song of God's love does not. It will continue on, long past the time when anyone remembers the story which I have told herein. I have owed much to the people who have told me their stories, to those who have given their lives for others, to those who form the hands and feet of the Body of Christ in the world around us. I hope that my story has returned some of that debt and inspired you who have read this. And remember to share your stories of the love of God in your life, for you are an important note in this song of God's love.

Order Form

To order copies of *Dancing into Joy: Transforming Our Darkness into Light* using a credit card, go to our website at www.dewspirit.com. To pay with check or money order, send this form with payment to: DewSpirit Publishing, PO Box 1208, Dickinson, ND 58601.

Your name: _____

Address: _____
City, State,
and Zip: _____

Phone #: _____

Please send me _____copies of *Dancing into Joy* at $14.95

each for a total of   _____
Add $3.00 for shipping and
handling of first book   _____

Plus $1.00 for each additional book   _____

North Dakota residents add sales tax_____

                Total   _____

For information concerning the Dancing into Joy Workbook (due out fall 2006) and discounts for multiple copy orders see our webpage at www.DewSpirit.com. We also plan to sell note cards by the cover artist of the original cover on our site. Other discounts available online, as well as creative writing by Spirit, Kathleen's loyal canine companion.

About the Author

While *Dancing Into Joy* is Kathleen Chesnut's first book, it is not her first venture into print. This was at the College of Mount Saint Vincent in Riverdale, New York, where she edited the college paper. Later in seminary, she won the 1992 Mercersburg Society Prize with her paper that was published in the New Mercersburg Review.

As a volunteer teacher at the Red Cloud Indian School in Pine Ridge, South Dakota, Kathleen coached the drama club that won a district competition. On the Rosebud Reservation she helped high school students create a literary magazine. When a fellow teacher commented that an English class which Kathleen had taught they year before 'didn't know their grammar, but sure could think', Kathleen felt herself to be successful, believing that students empowered to think for themselves could go forth to learn anything they need to know.

After leaving the Roman Catholic Church, she joined a local United Methodist church. Then, in her 30's, heeding the call to ministry, she joined the United Church of Christ, a denomination that encourages its people to think for themselves. Kathleen transferred to Lancaster Theological Seminary to learn more about her new denomination, and graduated in 1992, and was ordained in 1993.

Rev. M. Kathleen Chesnut has pastored churches in Rennsselaer, New York, and in the communities of Pomeroy and Fonda in Iowa. She now lives in North Dakota serving as pastor for two churches - First Congregational Church in Dickinson, and First Presbyterian Church in Belfield.

Praise for Dancing into Joy

"*Dancing into Joy* is an invitation to join Rev. Kathleen Chesnut on a sacred journey of life. A journey that begins in the depths of pain and fright and meanders its way to the mountaintop of greatest joy. Rev. Chesnut holds before us a faith filled life, asking us to join with her in the experience of its pain, the exploration of its strength, the reception of its hope and the dance in its light. I found this sacred journey to be a source of inspiration as I shared with her the experience of the God that embraced her."
Wade Schemmel, Conference Minister, Northern Plains Conference of the United Church of Christ

This heartfelt book is the story of God's gifts of love and joy and the human journey from darkness into light. Through prose, poetry and a combination of both Kathleen a United Church of Christ minister, expresses her life experiences. Through her Inner five year old she connects to her personal, inner knowing and learns her lessons of healing. The story of faith has long been a church principle, and Kathleen weaves her own magic from the past into the present, making this a story of joy for all times.
Shamai Currim PhD
Psychotherapist

"*Dancing into Joy* offers a taste of resurrection - a liberation from the grave clothes of its author's victimized childhood, from the frozen loneliness of distrust, from a political and economic system that destroys community, from the ashes of 9/11. And it offers a taste of resurrection into the joyful love of God that continually increases the more we give it away. In a medley of memoir, meditation, poetry, letter, fiction, sermon, mythology and essay, Kathleen Chesnut gives her readers a chance to join in a communal, spiraling Easter dance."

Virginia Ramey Mollenkott, Ph.D. author or co-author of 13 books, including *Omnigender: A Trans-religious Approach*

"Kathleen Chesnut's gift to us is her deep love of God and her willingness to share that love with us. Her spiritual journey takes us thru her childhood pain and trauma and brings the light of God to these deep pains. It gives one hope and courage in our own lives and brings us closer to the Divine. It is truly a balance between light and dark. An uplifting and delightful book."

Martha Piesco Hoff, a graduate of the Barbara Brennan School of healing, is a medical intuitive and healer. She is cofounder and director of the Fire and Wind Healing Institute

Printed in the United States
88556LV00001B/67-138/A